Free Video  **Free Video**

Essential Test Tips Video from Trivium Test Prep

Dear Customer,

Thank you for purchasing from Trivium Test Prep! We're honored to help you prepare for your MBLEx exam.

To show our appreciation, we're offering a **FREE *MBLEx Essential Test Tips* Video by Trivium Test Prep**.* Our video includes 35 test preparation strategies that will make you successful on the MBLEx. All we ask is that you email us your feedback and describe your experience with our product. Amazing, awful, or just so-so: we want to hear what you have to say!

To receive your **FREE *MBLEx Essential Test Tips* Video**, please email us at 5star@triviumtestprep.com. Include "Free 5 Star" in the subject line and the following information in your email:

1. The title of the product you purchased.
2. Your rating from 1 – 5 (with 5 being the best).
3. Your feedback about the product, including how our materials helped you meet your goals and ways in which we can improve our products.
4. Your full name and shipping address so we can send your **FREE *MBLEx Essential Test Tips* Video**.

If you have any questions or concerns please feel free to contact us directly at 5star@triviumtestprep.com.

Thank you!

- Trivium Test Prep Team

*To get access to the free video please email us at 5star@triviumtestprep.com, and please follow the instructions above.

MBLEx PRACTICE TESTS:

3 Full-Length Practice Exams with Detailed Answers for the Massage and Bodywork Licensing Examination

E. M. Falgout

Copyright © 2022 by Ascencia Test Prep

ISBN-13: 9781637980712

ALL RIGHTS RESERVED. By purchase of this book, you have been licensed one copy for personal use only. No part of this work may be reproduced, redistributed, or used in any form or by any means without prior written permission of the publisher and copyright owner. Ascencia Test Prep; Trivium Test Prep; Accepted, Inc.; and Cirrus Test Prep are all imprints of Trivium Test Prep, LLC.

The Federation of State Massage Therapy Boards was not involved in the creation or pro-duction of this product, is not in any way affiliated with Ascencia, and does not sponsor or endorse this product. All test names (and their acronyms) are trademarks of their respective owners. This study guide is for general information only and does not claim endorsement by any third party.

Image(s) used under license from Shutterstock.com

Table of Contents

Introduction i

1 Practice Test One 1
ANSWER KEY 13

2 Practice Test Two 25
ANSWER KEY 37

3 Practice Test Three 49
ANSWER KEY 60

INTRODUCTION: BECOMING A LICENSED MASSAGE THERAPIST

Congratulations! You are one step closer to becoming a certified massage therapist. The end of examinations is in sight, and soon your practice will be in full swing.

Before you can begin your practice as a professional massage therapist, there are a few more steps to complete following massage school graduation. The MBLEx (Massage and Bodywork Licensing Examination) is one of them. After you receive confirmation that you have passed the exam, you can begin the process to become licensed to practice in your state. The licensing process varies from state to state. The best information can be found with your state's regulatory board—either online or in person, via phone or at the office.

This book is designed to help you succeed in the examination and beyond. In this introductory chapter, you will learn what you can expect in preparing to take the MBLEx and what steps to take once you pass.

What is a Massage Therapist?

A **massage therapist** is a professional trained in the manipulation of soft tissues of the body by stroking, rubbing, kneading, and using other techniques to encourage relaxation and healing in the client's body.

There are many different types, or modalities, of massage that massage therapists can incorporate into their practice and treatments—typically massage therapists will use a blend of their knowledge and skills to create their own treatment style. Just like other professionals, massage therapists can use their unique brand to build a client base; whether you are known for your gentle, relaxing work or your deep, therapeutic work, or perhaps a mixture of both, clients will seek you out based on your style in addition to things like your personality, work ethic, and practice space.

To become a professional massage therapist working in the United States, an individual will have to fulfill a number of requirements as described below.

QUALIFICATIONS

Requirements to become a professional massage therapist vary from state to state, and sometimes even from county to county within a state. It is very important that you know and understand the rules where you live, or where you want to practice, to ensure you have met all the requirements to practice professionally. If you have questions about requirements, you can find specific resources at your school, or you can contact the regulatory oversight body/registrar of your state.

While students entering a massage school program are encouraged to have some secondary education or some degree of professional experience, a GED or high school diploma is all that most schools require.

Most massage schools offer programs that meet, if not exceed, hours and education required by their state for licensure, in addition to providing students with the knowledge to pass the MBLEx. Hours for general massage programs can vary from 350 hours to 1,000, depending on the state. Most programs only offer the bare minimum in regards to massage education, and often certifications like prenatal and postnatal massage or hot stone massage are obtained through continuing education after a massage therapist is a practicing professional.

In addition to classroom learning, most massage schools will offer on-the-job training with externships in sports offices or spas, student clinics, and other events outside school. Students can be observed by instructors and other professionals—allowing them to get some "real world" experience while still receiving coaching from the experts. Stay organized with the following checklist:

Becoming a Professional Massage Therapist: Checklist
- ☐ Complete massage school program.
- ☐ Study for the MBLEx.
- ☐ Pass the MBLEx.
- ☐ Register with the state and pay fees.
- ☐ Receive your license in the mail.
- ☐ Begin your professional practice!

COMMON ROLES AND RESPONSIBILITIES OF MASSAGE THERAPISTS

Being a professional massage therapist is an incredibly rewarding line of work. You get to help people who are stressed or in pain return to a more relaxed state of mind, teach them about their muscular anatomy and show them how to stretch to relieve chronically tight muscle groups, and become a constant sign of strength and peace in people's lives. It feels good!

As rewarding as the field of massage therapy can be, it also has challenges. Sometimes schedules are not right, or a person might forget his appointment; you might have a client who was not completely truthful on her intake form, or you may have a client who is inappropriate or difficult to deal with. While we always hope all clients will come fifteen minutes before their appointment, be honest with their health history, and behave kindly, we have to be prepared to deal professionally with the worst—just in case.

Excellent communication skills are of the utmost importance. You will not only appear professional, but you will also earn respect from your clients by setting boundaries. Keeping things professional can sometimes be difficult with very friendly clients who want to know more about you—where you grew up, where you live now, who you vote for, if you're seeing anyone... The slope can get slippery pretty quickly. Being an excellent communicator, though, you can put a stop to these comments and questions by encouraging clients to focus on their breathing, or, if that does not work, by asking them to stop or warning them you will have to stop the treatment if their prying continues.

The above is an example of being professional and keeping yourself safe. Other safety concerns may be physical; to avoid risking injury, make sure equipment is in working order and cords and other hazards are out of the way of both the client and the therapist. Communication protects clients by keeping them informed as long as you, as the therapist, describe the treatment specifically. (Please note this information is covered more in depth in chapter 3 of this review book.)

Not to be dismissed is hygiene, which is also of the utmost importance. You should maintain short, unpainted nails; keep hair out of your face; clean your body regularly; and wash your hands frequently throughout your shift, especially after each client. Also, keep in mind that what you eat emits smells from your body; if garlic chicken gives you gas, it is probably best to save that meal for after your shift is over.

> Think about it. A client is waiting for her massage therapist and sees him picking his nose or eating. Without washing his hands, the therapist greets her and takes her to the treatment room. Then, during the massage he blows his nose without washing his hands. Not only is that disgusting, but it also puts her at risk of catching a cold. She will probably complain to management and get the therapist scolded, suspended, or worse; she may even leave a negative review on social media. Either of those actions could cost the therapist not only his reputation, but also his career. You do not want to be that therapist.

The best way to deal with clients is to try to put yourself in their shoes. Yes, the client may be acting like a jerk, but on her intake form she said she has had lower back and neck pain for three months. You would probably be a little grumpy too if you were in pain that long. If all else fails, remain professional and know that after the treatment, you can suggest another therapist for her next massage.

Massage Therapy Settings

A number of people still view massage as a luxury that occurs in a high-end spa. While that can be the case, there are many different settings where massage takes place.

Yes, massage can take place in a high-priced, luxury spa. Typically, these massage treatments come with flourishes, or extras, such as body wraps or facials, or hot stone treatments. Because of the setting, the experience of the therapist, and additions to the treatment, these massages are often expensive, being upward of $150 per treatment. Not only can you work in spas on land, but cruise ships also have spas—you can see the world while working.

As you are currently studying massage therapy or have just completed your training, you know that massage is much more than a relaxing treatment at a spa. Massage can also take place in a rehabilitation clinic, for clients recovering from a physical injury or an addiction. As discussed in chapter 6, compassionate touch can promote healing and serenity within the body.

Massage can also supplement chiropractic and physical therapy as part of a monthly maintenance regimen or as a temporary measure during recovering from an injury or surgery. In addition, professional and collegiate sports teams often have massage therapists on staff to ensure their players are in top-notch condition both before and after sporting events.

Sports massage, deep tissue, clinical/medical massage, oncology (cancer) massage—all of these specific, different types of massage are needed in a number of settings. Massage therapy is a growing field with a wide range of opportunity and advancement in a number of different areas.

In addition to the physical practice of performing massage, there are plenty of other jobs within massage, from teaching general massage courses or continuing education classes to writing about massage for magazines or even test preparation books like this one. The world of massage is rich with possibilities!

The Future of Massage Therapy

The world of massage is far reaching and ever expanding. As the field gains more credibility with national certification standards like the MBLEx and state licensing, opportunities for therapists grow. Some insurance carriers even cover massage therapy in clinical settings; due to the affordability of such coverage, more people are being drawn to massage as clients. Additionally, many clients are looking for a holistic health approach, using massage along with a healthy diet and exercise to maintain a balanced lifestyle.

Furthermore, medical professionals are increasingly looking to massage therapists to help their patients with pain management or in palliative care, though there are some out there who still view massage as a luxury.

While it is great news for you as a therapist that the world of massage therapy is growing and advancing, it also means that with the change and growth will come new challenges. Therapists are responsible for individual professional development. More reputable institutions are turning out massage therapists ready to grow and advance the industry. Massage therapists must uphold a high level of professionalism to maintain and increase the respect and validity paid to the field and their work.

National Certification

Massage, like any other trade profession, needs to have rules, regulations, and standards of education that can be measured to ensure that individual professionalism is maintained. The MBLEx is the national certification that measures these standards in the world of massage.

What is the MBLEx?

The MBLEx is maintained and administered by the Federation of State Massage Therapy Boards (FSMTB). The FSMTB's mission is to support member boards in the work so that the practice of massage therapy is provided to the public in a safe and effective manner. The FSMTB developed the MBLEx to "offer the first standardized licensing exam for the massage and bodywork profession; to facilitate professional mobility; to give the regulatory community oversight over exam content, organizational policies and procedures pertaining to the exam; and to significantly speed up the process between application and examination to avoid unnecessary delays in licensure."

Think of it like this: passing the MBLEx and getting licensed establishes your credibility as a massage therapist in your community. Your clients will see your credentials and be confident that you know what you are doing in providing their treatment.

There are two different ways to sign up to take the MBLEx: through the FSMTB or through your state's licensing board or agency. To go through the FSMTB, sign up for the exam at the official website: https://www.fsmtb.org/mblex/application-process/. After you verify that you have completed all the necessary education, agree to the test's policies in writing, and pay the fee of $195, you'll receive an "Authorization to Test" (ATT) via email. You must sign up to take the test within ninety days at Pearson Vue: http://www.pearsonvue.com/fsmtb/. If you need to change locations or your testing date, you can contact Pearson Vue as well.

Should you go through your state's licensing board or agency, you must first be approved by that organization; the same steps as above apply in terms of signing off on the test, paying the fee, and scheduling the exam.

Each multiple-choice question is worth one raw point. The total number of questions you answer correctly is added up to obtain your raw score, which is then converted to a number on a scale of 300 – 900. In order to pass the MBLEx, you must receive at least a score of 630.

The score will be kept electronically, but you can request a physical copy for a twenty-dollar fee.

Either route you take will allow you to move toward being a licensed professional therapist after you pass—it really just depends on how your school or state does things. One option is no better than the other; what you choose may be based on preference and availability of services in your area.

What You Need to Learn to Pass the MBLEx

The breakdown of the exam follows in the table below. While it may seem like an overwhelming amount of information, there are only 100 questions to be answered in two hours. Think back to your days in massage school, and use this test prep as a road map for your success.

Everything from muscle actions, origins, and insertions to asking your clients about their health history will be on the exam. Remember to breathe.

What's on the MBLEx?

Topic	Content	Percentage	Number of Questions*
Body Systems	Anatomy and Physiology	11%	10 – 12
	Kinesiology	12%	11 – 13
Pathology	Pathology, Contraindications, Special Populations, Areas of Caution	14%	13 – 16
Application	Benefits and Physiological Effects of Techniques That Manipulate Soft Tissue	15%	16 – 17
Assessment	Client Assessment, Reassessment, and Treatment Planning	17%	16 – 18
Professional	Ethics, Boundaries, Laws, Regulations	16%	16 – 18
	Guidelines for Professional Practice	15%	14 – 17

*numbers are approximate

What to Expect on Testing Day

You do not have to dread test day anymore! You have put hours, days, weeks, and months into preparing for this exam, and this book is designed to make sure you know your stuff—which you do!

Now that you know you have the material down, here is what you need to know for the logistical side of taking this exam:

- Arrive at least thirty minutes early in the event there is a delay, and to ensure you are not feeling rushed before the start of the exam.
- Bring only what you need. Most things, such as a watch, phone, chewing gum, etc., will not be allowed into the exam room. Lockers will be provided for keys or jackets.
- Two forms of valid identification are required. Check https://www.fsmtb.org/ to be sure you have the most up-to-date information.

You will not be able to flag questions for review at a later time. If you need to use the bathroom, you may raise your hand, but it is better to go before the exam begins as the time does not stop for your breaks.

Since the test is computerized, it will base your questions on how well you are doing in the exam. If you answer a question correctly, then the next question will be of the same or higher difficulty level, but if you answer a question incorrectly, the following question will be easier. This pattern continues throughout the test.

After answering 100 questions in (under) two hours, you can notify the official that you are finished with the exam, and your score will be waiting for you at the front where you checked in.

After You Pass the MBLEx

You did it! You are now a CMT, or certified massage therapist. Now you have to register with your state licensing board so you can practice professionally. Most states require licenses to be renewed every two years, for a fee, in addition to a certain number of continuing education (CE) hours. As always, it is important to check with your state licensing board to make sure you have everything necessary for the initial license and then for the following renewal years.

Continuing education courses allow you to build your skill set and open your practice to a new level of clientele. Also, it is good for professionals to constantly be learning and practicing their skills on other professionals to get productive feedback.

The world of professional massage therapy is now open to you! Go forth and prosper!

ONE: Practice Test One

Read the question carefully and choose the most correct answer.

1. How long should a massage therapist keep a client's records?
   A) one month
   B) ten days
   C) three years
   D) ten years

2. What is the name of the circulatory system function that delivers nutrients and oxygen to tissues and organs and also collects cell waste from interstitial fluids?
   A) hypophyseal
   B) diastolic
   C) capillary exchange
   D) hepatic portal

3. A professional organization provides all of the following services except one. Which one?
   A) legal representation for members
   B) a code of ethics
   C) legislative updates affecting the profession
   D) public awareness

4. The book *The Art of Massage* was published by whom?
   A) Douglas O. Graham
   B) John Harvey Kellogg
   C) Aulus Cornelius Celsus
   D) Pehr Henrik Ling

5. Which of the following is NOT a benefit of massage?
   A) decreased cortisol levels
   B) increased heart rate
   C) increased oxytocin levels
   D) decreased sympathetic nervous system firings

6. Filtrate is a fluid in the urinary system. Which of the following is *true* about filtrate?
   A) Ninety-nine percent is urinated out of the body.
   B) One percent is retained by the body.
   C) Filtrate primarily consists of toxic waste.
   D) Most filtrate is reabsorbed.

7. What are the two primary lymphatic structures?
   A) spleen and vermiform appendix
   B) afferent and efferent lymphatic vessels
   C) right lymphatic duct and thoracic duct
   D) bone marrow and the thymus

8. Which cranial nerve is related to tongue movement?
   A) trochlear
   B) facial
   C) olfactory
   D) hypoglossal

9. Which of the following is a set of limits that defines and maintains a relationship?
   A) nonverbal cues
   B) licenses
   C) designations
   D) boundaries

10. What does the acronym SOAP stand for in SOAP notes?
    A) Subjective Obtain Act Plan
    B) Subjective Objective Assessment Plan
    C) Sound Off All Parties
    D) Subjective Objective Ask Plan

11. Who or what is amma?
    A) the first formal written record of Chinese medical practices
    B) the Yellow Emperor of China
    C) a system of manual and energy techniques
    D) a Greek word for rubbing

12. Which of the following is a skin condition resulting from rapid replication of epithelial cells?
    A) mole
    B) wart
    C) eczema
    D) psoriasis

13. Who should NOT receive a full-body massage?
    A) a client with fibromyalgia
    B) a lonely client
    C) an angry client
    D) a client with hypertension

14. When therapists receive telephone calls from potential clients, they should do what?
    A) be present and enthusiastic
    B) explain the fee schedule first
    C) relate their skills and abilities
    D) explain their hours up front so they can establish boundaries at the outset

15. Which is the yang organ of digestion that peaks from 9 p.m. to 11 p.m.? Its element is fire, and it has twenty-three acupressure points.
    A) triple warmer
    B) pericardium
    C) stomach
    D) bladder

16. Which of the following is NOT a principle of massage?
    A) deep-superficial-deep
    B) general-specific-general
    C) peripheral-central-peripheral
    D) proximal-distal-proximal

17. What term did Hippocrates use to classify phlegm, blood, yellow bile, and black bile?

- **A)** Hellenic
- **B)** anatripsis
- **C)** systematic principles of diagnosis
- **D)** the four humors

18. Each of the following options list two things a state may require or specify, except one. Which one?

- **A)** hours of education, US citizenship
- **B)** designation, license renewal requirements
- **C)** accepted exam, liability insurance
- **D)** CPR training, certificate of health

19. Bolus and chyme are associated with which body system?

- **A)** reproductive
- **B)** endocrine
- **C)** urinary
- **D)** digestive

20. What should be included in the *S* of a SOAP note?

- **A)** symptoms the client talks about
- **B)** things the therapist sees on the client
- **C)** signs of injury
- **D)** scheduling issues

21. What is fascia?

- **A)** Fascia is a muscle that lies just under the dermis.
- **B)** Fascia is a connective tissue that only covers bones.
- **C)** Fascia is a connective tissue that covers everything from blood vessels to muscles.
- **D)** Fascia is a ligament sheath.

22. Regarding burns, which statement is NOT correct?

- **A)** A first-degree burn is considered relatively minor.
- **B)** A third-degree burn results in the most pain.
- **C)** A fourth-degree burn may be diagnosed if the damage reaches tendon and bone.
- **D)** A second-degree burn may require a skin graft.

23. Inspiration occurs when the pressure within what structures falls below the atmospheric pressure?

- **A)** maxillary sinus
- **B)** nasal cavity
- **C)** alveolar sacs
- **D)** bronchioles

24. What stages does the client's body go through when receiving a cold treatment?

- **A)** burning, tingling, cold, numbness
- **B)** numbness, cold, tingling, burning
- **C)** cold, burning, tingling, numbness
- **D)** cold, tingling, burning, numbness

25. If self-disclosure during massage sessions moves from a client sharing information that is pertinent to the massage to revealing personal information that is unrelated to the massage, what might be the outcome?

- **A)** The therapist-client bond becomes stronger.
- **B)** The therapist begins to consider pursuing a new career as a psychologist.
- **C)** The client will keep coming back because the therapist is such a good listener.
- **D)** The therapist begins to feel resentful and burned out.

26. Which of the following is NOT true about Pehr Henrik Ling?
   A) He was a Swedish physician.
   B) He opened the Swedish Royal Central Institute of Gymnastics.
   C) He created the Swedish movement cure.
   D) He is considered the father of physical therapy.

27. What happens to the body in the parasympathetic nervous system?
   A) decreased heart rate, increased digestion, inhibited saliva
   B) increased heart rate, decreased digestion, decreased saliva
   C) decreased heart rate, relaxed bladder, increased digestion
   D) decreased heart rate, increased digestion, contracted bladder

28. What is NOT one of the best ways to become competent in a modality?
   A) taking a weekend workshop
   B) understanding the relationship between anatomy and physiology and the modality
   C) familiarizing oneself with evidence-based studies
   D) a genuine belief the therapy will do no harm

29. What should be included in the O of a SOAP note?
   A) obtuse information
   B) oblique pain
   C) observed information
   D) obvious information

30. Which statement is NOT true about chakra balancing?
   A) Chakras are energy channels that function separately.
   B) Chakras' energy channels are located along the midline.
   C) Colors associated with chakras are formed by vibrational frequencies and wavelengths.
   D) Chakra energy channels are associated with organs, systems, and anatomical locations.

31. If a therapist is almost 100 percent certain a coworker is gathering personal information from client files, what should he do?
   A) He should approach the coworker and ask her what the heck she is doing.
   B) Do nothing. It is not up to the therapist to police his coworkers.
   C) He should call the state board and report his suspicions.
   D) He should tell his supervisor what he thinks his coworker is doing and why he came to that conclusion.

32. What is an inflammatory bowel disease that affects the large intestine and rectum sections of the colon?
   A) ulcerative colitis
   B) Crohn's disease
   C) celiac disease
   D) goiter

33. Which of the following is NOT true of an effleurage stroke?
   A) It is a gliding stroke.
   B) It distributes lotion.
   C) It assesses muscle tone and tightness.
   D. Techniques include tapping and plucking.

34. What is a blood-borne pathogen?
    A) an infectious microorganism in human blood that can cause disease
    B) an infectious microorganism in plants
    C) a deadly pathogen in the air that gets in blood
    D) anything that carries germs

35. Which of the following terms is NOT related to proprioceptive neuromuscular facilitation (PNF) treatment?
    A) slow twitch
    B) spiral-diagonal
    C) hold-relax stretch
    D) contract-relax stretch

36. Peyer's patches and tonsils are most closely associated with which body system?
    A) immune
    B) digestive
    C) lymphatic
    D) endocrine

37. If a client arrives for a massage drunk, the therapist can refuse to massage based on what?
    A) personal safety
    B) contraindications
    C) improper hygiene
    D) revulsion to the smell of alcohol

38. All but one of the following massage modalities were developed by osteopaths. Which one?
    A) polarity therapy
    B) visceral manipulation
    C) zero balancing
    D) Watsu

39. Who benefits from massage?
    A) everyone
    B) only babies
    C) everyone but babies
    D) everyone but the elderly

40. What are the two types of myofibrils?
    A) actin and myosin
    B) troponin and tropomyosin
    C) ADP and ATP
    D) epimysium and perimysium

41. If a client writes on an intake form that she had cancer treatment years ago and fully recovered, what is a logical question?
    A) "Did you ask your doctor if it is okay to get a massage?"
    B) "Did you have any lymph nodes removed in the course of treatment?"
    C) "Do you have a family history of cancer?"
    D) "Was your recovery difficult for you and your family?"

42. What should be included in the A of a SOAP note?
    A) actions of the client
    B) actions of the therapist
    C) a new idea about the client's issue
    D) a recommendation for a new therapist

43. What is the name of the sphincter that is located at the junction of the stomach and small intestine?
    A) lower esophageal
    B) sphincter of Oddi
    C) ileocecal
    D) pyloric

44. All of the following EXCEPT one are concepts and terminology found in a professional code of ethics. Which one?
    A) a commitment to competence
    B) honesty and integrity
    C) annually renewing membership to maintain a professional license
    D) confidentiality of client information

45. What happens to the body in the sympathetic nervous system?
    A) increased heart rate, constricted airways, decreased digestion
    B) increased heart rate, relaxed airways, secretion of epinephrine
    C) increased heart rate, contracted bladder, increased digestion
    D) increased heart rate, increased digestion, relaxed airways

46. Which statement is NOT correct?
    A) Lymphatic trunks feed into the right lymphatic duct and the thoracic duct.
    B) The cisterna chyli collects lymph draining from the abdomen and lower body.
    C) The vermiform appendix is the most important secondary lymphatic structure.
    D) The spleen has only afferent lymphatic vessels.

47. What is the importance of keeping and maintaining SOAP notes?
    A) to instruct on how to clean laundry
    B) to know how to better treat other clients
    C) to keep for a therapist's scrapbook
    D) to list clients' issues and track their progress

48. In massage therapy, when is NOT getting informed consent okay?
    A) when a client runs late for an appointment, for the purpose of giving a client as much hands-on massage time as possible
    B) when a client gets weekly massages and it is just not necessary anymore
    C) never
    D) when a client is deaf

49. If a client begins to cry and discloses that he has been really depressed and is considering suicide, what is the therapist's obligation?
    A) A massage therapist is bound by rules of confidentiality and cannot disclose this threat.
    B) The therapist should end the massage immediately and call 911.
    C) The therapist should listen attentively and be empathetic.
    D) When the massage is over, the therapist should immediately call the National Suicide Prevention Lifeline and ask for advice and guidance.

50. Which type of joint is classified as slightly movable?
    A) synarthrotic
    B) diarthrotic
    C) synovial
    D) amphiarthrotic

51. Which of the following is a corticosteroid?
    A) Januvia®
    B) Metformin
    C) prednisone
    D) lisinopril

52. A modality of massage and bodywork that includes balancing energy flow, attunements, and sacred symbols is called what?

- **A)** Reiki
- **B)** craniosacral
- **C)** lomi lomi
- **D)** raindrop technique

53. What is a benefit of percussion?

- **A)** to feel the beat
- **B)** to warm up muscles
- **C)** to stimulate muscles
- **D)** to cause the client to bleed

54. Legally, who can provide massage in a professional setting?

- **A)** anyone
- **B)** a licensed massage therapist
- **C)** a licensed esthetician
- **D)** a sports coach

55. There are two types of immune responses, innate and adaptive. Which body system is most closely associated with the adaptive response?

- **A)** digestive
- **B)** integumentary
- **C)** lymphatic
- **D)** respiratory

56. Continually attempting to engage with the therapist socially is a sign of what psychological occurrence?

- **A)** transference
- **B)** dual relationship
- **C)** contraindication
- **D)** sexual misconduct

57. The autonomic nervous system is broken down into which two subcategories?

- **A)** brain and spinal cord
- **B)** central and peripheral nervous systems
- **C)** parasympathetic and sympathetic
- **D)** somatic and brain

58. In traditional Chinese medicine, which element represents late summer and nurturing?

- **A)** water
- **B)** earth
- **C)** metal
- **D)** wood

59. Transference may trigger what?

- **A)** a nonverbal cue from a client
- **B)** a job promotion
- **C)** countertransference
- **D)** a written warning from a supervisor to an employee

60. What should be included in the *P* of a SOAP note?

- **A)** patient information
- **B)** palliative care
- **C)** plans for future treatments
- **D)** performance review

61. What is NOT the description of a trigger point?

- **A)** a hyperirritable spot in a taut band of muscle
- **B)** a tense area that radiates pain when activated
- **C)** an area of discomfort otherwise known as a knot
- **D)** a hyperirritable spot near the tendon of a muscle

62. If a new client arrives for an appointment, the therapist should do what?
   A) shout from another room that she is busy with a client so the newcomer will think she has a busy practice
   B) greet the client with a hug and tell her that she has come to the right place
   C) give the client a form to fill out and tell her you will return in five or ten minutes
   D) greet the client courteously, give her the intake form, and tell her you will be available if she has any questions

63. What does "being safe" mean for a massage therapist?
   A) looking both ways before crossing the street
   B) planning an evacuation in the event of emergency
   C) identifying and controlling hazards and risks
   D) identifying and addressing pain

64. What is the term used to identify a muscle that opposes a movement?
   A) synergist
   B) antagonist
   C) prime mover
   D) fixator

65. Which of the following is true about shamans?
   A) Illness and disease were believed to be caused by shamans.
   B) Shamans were considered to be evil.
   C) Shamans were considered to be healers in their tribes.
   D) Only male members of tribes were shamans.

66. What is hydrotherapy?
   A) therapy using firemen's hoses
   B) therapy on a table in a pool
   C) therapy using water in any of its forms to achieve therapeutic effect
   D) therapy using no water

67. The clavicle articulates with the manubrium forming what joint?
   A) glenohumeral
   B) sternoclavicular
   C) acromioclavicular
   D) acetabulofemoral

68. Which of the following is NOT true of a contraindication?
   A) A contraindication implies that no massage may be performed.
   B) Pitted edema is a site-specific contraindication.
   C) An aneurysm is a condition that would not benefit from a Swedish massage.
   D) A client with a medical condition that is in an acute state should not receive a massage.

69. What is effleurage?
   A) Effleurage is to knead.
   B) Effleurage is to glide, stroke, or touch lightly.
   C) Effleurage is to use friction deep in the muscle belly.
   D) Effleurage is to stroke in a deep, rhythmic, and slow manner.

70. How do trigger points develop?
   A) shooting a gun
   B) repetitive activity or injury
   C) blood flow to the area backs up
   D) standing for long periods of time

71. A fifteen-year-old boy who is on the soccer team at school comes to a therapist for a massage with parental consent. During the massage the client grimaces when the therapist massages his upper arm. The therapist expresses concern and asks if the pressure is okay. The client replies that in the locker room after a game his coach grabbed his arm and told him his mistake cost the game. What should the massage therapist do?
    A) The therapist should tell the boy she is sorry about what happened.
    B) She feels really bad, but what can she do? It is up to his parents to deal with this issue.
    C) The therapist should avoid the area and, when the massage is complete, communicate with the parents about what their son disclosed and then follow up with a call to social services.
    D) The therapist should excuse herself from the massage and contact social services immediately.

72. The brain's hypothalamus prompts which part of the pituitary gland to release, and inhibit its release of, hormones?
    A the cortex
    B) the anterior lobe
    C) the posterior lobe
    D) the medulla

73. What is kneading?
    A) Kneading is to stroke gently.
    B) Kneading is to pick up the muscle and pull away from the body.
    C) Kneading is to pick up the muscle and move in a circular, squeezing compression.
    D) Kneading is to squeeze the AC joint.

74. Which of the following refers to an outward bulge in a vein, artery, or the heart itself caused by weakening of the vessel wall usually due to hypertension?
    A) arteriosclerosis
    B) aneurysm
    C) hernia
    D) decubitus ulcer

75. Erector spinae muscles consist of three columns of muscles. Which three are they?
    A) external oblique, internal oblique, transverse abdominis
    B) iliocostalis, longissimus, spinalis
    C) external intercostals, internal intercostals, serratus posterior inferior
    D) lateral pterygoid, medial pterygoid, masseter

76. What is percussion?
    A) It is performed with the idea to shake the client.
    B) It is performed with the idea of client as drum skin.
    C) Performed lightly or heavily, it helps to wake up the sleeping client.
    D) Performed lightly or heavily, it helps to stimulate muscles or loosen mucus.

77. A therapist has an arrangement with an accountant to provide massages in exchange for accounting services. What is this type of arrangement called?
    A) trading
    B) bartering
    C) inappropriate
    D) risky

78. Synapses, Schwann cells, and the sodium-potassium pump are most closely associated with which system?
    A) reproductive
    B) nervous
    C) urinary
    D) muscular

79.. Which of the statements pertaining to the Ayurvedic approach is NOT true?
    A) Most illness begins during the digestive process.
    B) People should avoid caustic environments.
    C) Ingesting more liquids than solids is necessary.
    D) Adapting seasonally is important.

80. What is a contraindication to pregnancy massage?
    A) any work in the first trimester
    B) the pregnant woman is going into labor
    C) any work in the second trimester
    D) the pregnant woman is on bed rest under a doctor's care

81. Which of the following is NOT a type of massage?
    A) sports massage
    B) lymphatic drainage massage
    C) acrobatic massage
    D) Swedish massage

82. What Swedish massage technique is described as similar to wringing out a wet rag?
    A) vibration
    B) raking
    C) friction
    D) tapotement

83. What is a potential benefit of a social media dual relationship?
    A) finding a new friend with common social interests
    B) discovering a client is going to the same concert as the therapist and maybe meeting up
    C) a client discovering the therapist is a member of the state massage board
    D) a client finding out the therapist's sister is dating someone she used to date and getting filled in on his bad behavior

84. What is a hydrocollator?
    A) a heat therapy of gel-filled packs stored in a hot water tank
    B) water treatment
    C) hot therapy used with stones
    D) a cold therapy applied with towels

85. Alpha and beta cells are most closely associated with which body system?
    A) endocrine
    B) integumentary
    C) nervous
    D) reproductive

86. Which layer of the epidermis is held in place by a basement membrane?
    A) stratum basale
    B) stratum lucidum
    C) stratum corneum
    D) stratum spinosum

87. Which of the following is NOT caused by a virus?
    A) HIV
    B) acne
    C) herpes simplex
    D) shingles

88. Who is considered the "father" of medicine?
    A) Herodicus
    B) Johann Mezger
    C) Hippocrates
    D) Asclepius

89. A therapist's friend refers a coworker for a massage. Once the therapist starts massaging the coworker regularly, the friend starts asking questions about where he lives, his age, and if he has a girlfriend. What should the therapist do?
    A) give all the details
    B) respond with anger and disgust that the friend would ask those questions
    C) tell the client
    D) tell the friend the therapist appreciates the referral but does not disclose personal information about clients

90. Why should a therapist work proximal-distal-proximal when massaging a limb?
    A) It helps to pump and flush the blood and lymph flow without backups.
    B) It helps to keep the therapist focused.
    C) It helps to keep the client awake during treatment.
    D) The principle has been passed down, but has lost its meaning.

91. What is referred to as the anatomical pacemaker?
    A) the sinoatrial node
    B) the atrioventricular node
    C) the heart's conduction system
    D) the sphygmomanometer

92. The sliding filament theory is associated with which body system?
    A) muscular
    B) skeletal
    C) nervous
    D) digestive

93. What is a proper height for a massage table?
    A) three feet above the ground
    B) at the therapist's shoulders
    C) whatever the therapist finds comfortable for work
    D) wherever the client feels comfortable

94. A therapist-client role presents itself as a what?
    A) mutual relationship
    B) fair balance of power
    C) business agreement
    D) role and power differential

95. What is homeostasis?
    A) the ability of the body to regulate equilibrium or balance across all systems
    B) the ability of the body to destroy equilibrium or balance across all systems
    C) the ability of the body to stay awake for twenty-four hours
    D) the ability of the body to ignore headaches

96. Which is an example of a convergent muscle?
    A) biceps brachii
    B) extensor digitorum longus
    C) rectus abdominis
    D) pectoralis major

97. The first time a client comes to a therapist for a massage she complains about lower back pain she has had for months. How should the therapist communicate when inquiring about this pain?

- **A)** "Oh, you probably have an issue with a lumbar vertebra putting pressure on the sciatic nerve. I can fix that."
- **B)** "Have you spoken with a doctor about this pain?"
- **C)** "You have such large breasts. This is probably contributing to your lower back pain."
- **D)** "I bet you sit all day at a computer."

98. What is the importance of working centripetally?

- **A)** to encourage bone growth
- **B)** to encourage the body to metabolize
- **C)** to encourage blood flow back to the heart
- **D)** to encourage the bladder to contract

99. How many times can sheets be reused before washing?

- **A)** once
- **B)** twice
- **C)** never
- **D)** all day

100. Arterioles, capillaries, and venules are most closely associated with which body system?

- **A)** circulatory
- **B)** lymphatic
- **C)** integumentary
- **D)** nervous

PRACTICE TEST ONE ANSWER KEY

1.
- A) Incorrect. A client's records should be kept for ten years.
- B) Incorrect. Ten days is not long enough to keep a client's records.
- C) Incorrect. Three years is seven years too short for keeping a client's records.
- **D) Correct.** A therapist should keep a client's records for ten years.

2.
- A) Incorrect. The hypophyseal is a portal system between the hypothalamus and anterior pituitary for the purpose of hormone exchange.
- B) Incorrect. Diastolic is a measure obtained when the ventricle relaxes.
- **C) Correct.** Capillary exchange is a circulatory system function performed by capillaries.
- D) Incorrect. The hepatic portal is a system that dumps collected blood into the liver, allowing it to extract glucose, fat, and proteins.

3.
- **A) Correct.** Providing legal representation to individual members is not a role of a professional organization.
- B) Incorrect. A code of ethics establishes consistency in how members practice.
- C) Incorrect. Professional organizations are a valuable source of information regarding pending legislation related to the profession.
- D) Incorrect. Communicating with the public can enhance and promote a profession.

4.
- A) Incorrect. Douglas O. Graham is best known for his publication entitled *A Practical Treatise on Massage: Its History, Mode of Application and Effects, Indications & Contra-Indications*.
- **B) Correct.** Kellogg's *The Art of Massage* was published in 1895.
- C) Incorrect. Aulus Cornelius Celsus was a Roman physician who wrote *De Medicina*.
- D) Incorrect. Pehr Henrik Ling died in 1839.

5.
- A) Incorrect. Massage does decrease cortisol (stress) levels.
- **B) Correct.** Massage decreases heart rate and encourages relaxation.
- C) Incorrect. Massage does increase oxytocin levels.
- D) Incorrect. Massage does decrease sympathetic nervous system (fight-or-flight) firings.

6.
- A) Incorrect. Ninety-nine percent of filtrate is reabsorbed and put back into circulation.
- B) Incorrect. One percent of filtrate is toxic waste and is removed from the body.
- C) Incorrect. Filtrate contains many things that can be used by the body.
- **D) Correct.** Most filtrate is reabsorbed.

7.
- A) Incorrect. The spleen and vermiform appendix are secondary lymphatic structures.
- B) Incorrect. Afferent vessels feed lymph into lymph nodes, and efferent vessels transport lymph out of lymph nodes.
- C) Incorrect. The right lymphatic and thoracic ducts drain lymph.
- **D) Correct.** Bone marrow produces B lymphocytes that stay in the marrow and mature and T lymphocytes that travel to the thymus and then mature.

8.
- A) Incorrect. The trochlear nerve is related to eye movements.
- B) Incorrect. The facial nerve is related to expressions, taste, and the production of saliva.
- C) Incorrect. The olfactory nerve is related to smell.
- **D) Correct.** The hypoglossal is related to tongue movement.

9.
- A) Incorrect. Nonverbal cues are expressions and reactions that suggest a positive or negative reaction.

- B) Incorrect. A license is given to someone who has met requirements and standards.
- C) Incorrect. A designation is a formal title given after requirements are met.
- **D) Correct.** In massage, boundaries are established by present rules, values, and morals.

10.
- A) Incorrect. *Obtain* and *act* are not the O and A of SOAP notes.
- **B) Correct.** *SOAP* stands for *Subjective Objective Assessment Plan*.
- C) Incorrect. This is not what SOAP notes stands for.
- D) Incorrect. The A in the acronym stands for *assessment*, not *ask*.

11.
- A) Incorrect. The Nei Ching is the formal written record of Chinese medical practices.
- B) Incorrect. Huang Ti was known as the Yellow Emperor of China. The Nei Ching was written during his period of rule.
- **C) Correct.** Amma is considered the forerunner of the practice of massage and bodywork.
- D) Incorrect. Hippocrates used the word *anatripsis* to refer to the technique of rubbing.

12.
- A) Incorrect. A mole is formed by an excessive amount of melanin.
- B) Incorrect. A wart is a small tumor that arises from the epidermis and is viral in nature.
- C) Incorrect. Eczema is believed to be tied to an internal systemic immune system dysfunction and its response to irritants and stress.
- **D) Correct.** Psoriasis appears as pink and red scaly patches.

13.
- A) Incorrect. Clients with fibromyalgia can benefit from different types of massage depending on their pain cycle.
- B) Incorrect. A lonely client would benefit from massage's social aspect and touch component.
- C) Incorrect. Angry clients can benefit from massage, which reduces stress levels and increases feel-good hormones.
- **D) Correct.** A client with hypertension (or high blood pressure) is at risk from a full-body massage because of the increased blood flow massage encourages.

14.
- **A) Correct.** The perception that you are listening and interested is important.
- B) Incorrect. This is an insulting way to begin a conversation.
- C) Incorrect. Let the client inquire about skills and abilities first.
- D) Incorrect. This will sound dismissive and aggressive.

15.
- **A) Correct.** The triple warmer has an upper, middle, and lower warmer section.
- B) Incorrect. The pericardium is a yin organ of circulation that peaks from 7 p.m. to 9 p.m., its element is fire, and it has nine acupressure points.
- C) Incorrect. The stomach is a yang organ of digestion that peaks from 7 a.m. to 9 a.m., its element is earth, and it has forty-five acupressure points.
- D) Incorrect. The bladder is a yang organ of digestion that peaks from 3 p.m. to 5 p.m., its element is water, and it has sixty-seven acupressure points.

16.
- **A) Correct.** The principle of massage is superficial-deep-superficial.
- B) Incorrect. General-specific-general is a principle of massage.
- C) Incorrect. Peripheral-central-peripheral is a principle of massage.
- D) Incorrect. Proximal-distal-proximal is a principle of massage.

17.
- A) Incorrect. The term *Hellenic* refers to a period in ancient Greece (also known as the *Classical Period*) when scientific study, art, philosophy, and literature flourished.
- B) Incorrect. *Anatripsis* was the term Hippocrates used to define rubbing.

C) Incorrect. Hippocrates did not use this term to classify bodily fluids.

D) **Correct.** Hippocrates referred to phlegm, blood, yellow bile, and black bile as the four humors.

18. A) **Correct.** A state may regulate hours of education required, but the federal government, not states, determines eligibility to practice a profession based on legal status in the United States.

B) Incorrect. A state can establish what title a massage therapist may use and license renewal requirements.

C) Incorrect. A state can determine which exam or exams a massage therapist must pass in order to obtain a license to practice. Also, some states require proof of liability insurance before a therapist can be licensed.

D) Incorrect. Most states require CPR training, and some may require a certificate of health from a physician.

19. A) Incorrect. There is no relationship at all.

B) Incorrect. There is no relationship at all.

C) Incorrect. There is no relationship at all.

D) **Correct.** A bolus is formed in the oral cavity, and chyme is a semifluid mass formed in the stomach.

20. A) **Correct.** Anything clients mention about their condition should be listed under S.

B) Incorrect. Things the therapist notices about the client should be listed under O.

C) Incorrect. Signs of injury would be listed in the O section.

D) Incorrect. Scheduling issues would not be included in SOAP notes.

21. A) Incorrect. Fascia is not a muscle.

B) Incorrect. Periosteum is a bone covering, not fascia.

C) **Correct.** Fascia is a connective tissue that covers everything from blood vessels to muscles.

D) Incorrect. Fascia is not a ligament sheath.

22. A) Incorrect. A first-degree burn only affects the epidermis.

B) **Correct.** If nerve damage results from a third-degree burn, pain will be diminished or nonexistent.

C) Incorrect. If burned skin results in damage to all three layers of skin and tendon and bone beneath, then a fourth-degree burn may be diagnosed.

D) Incorrect. Second-degree burns penetrate the dermis and may require a skin graft.

23. A) Incorrect. The maxillary is one of four sinuses in the upper respiratory system.

B) Incorrect. The right and left nostrils pull inhaled air into the nasal cavity.

C) **Correct.** The movement of air into and out of the lungs is because of a pressure gradient between the lungs and the atmosphere. Inspiration occurs when the pressure within the alveolar sacs falls below the atmospheric pressure, resulting in air entering the lungs.

D) Incorrect. The two bronchi branch into bronchioles that spread through each lung.

24. A) Incorrect. That is not the correct response order.

B) Incorrect. That is not the correct response order.

C) Incorrect. That is not the correct response order.

D) **Correct.** The client would feel cold, tingling, burning, and numbness during cold therapy.

25. A) Incorrect. There is no professional correlation between too much self-disclosure and the strengthening of the therapist-client bond.

B) Incorrect. While there is nothing wrong with pursuing a career as a psychologist, this thought has nothing to do with being a professional massage therapist.

C) Incorrect. Assuming this is a valid reason for a client to keep coming back diminishes the therapist's skills, training, and dedication.

PRACTICE TEST ONE ANSWER KEY 15

- D) **Correct.** Clients revealing too much personal information about themselves and their lives can become a huge burden for the therapist.

26. A) **Correct.** Pehr Henrik Ling was not a physician.
    B) Incorrect. He did open the Swedish Royal Central Institute of Gymnastics.
    C) Incorrect. The Swedish movement cure combined medical gymnastics, exercise, and massage.
    D) Incorrect. He is considered the father of physical therapy.

27. A) Incorrect. Saliva increases in the parasympathetic nervous system.
    B) Incorrect. Heart rate decreases and saliva production increases in the parasympathetic nervous system.
    C) Incorrect. The bladder contracts in the parasympathetic system.
    D) **Correct.** Heart rate decreases, digestion increases, and the bladder contracts in the parasympathetic nervous system.

28. A) **Correct.** Taking a weekend workshop in a new modality does not guarantee competence.
    B) Incorrect. Understanding the effect of a modality on human anatomy and physiology is valuable.
    C. Incorrect. Familiarizing yourself with evidence-based studies aids communicating the benefits of a modality.
    D) Incorrect. A genuine belief in a therapy will motivate a therapist to commit to and practice the application.

29. A) Incorrect. Unclear information should be clarified and filed accordingly.
    B) Incorrect. If the oblique muscles are in pain, that would be listed in the S section.
    C) **Correct.** Anything the therapist observes in the client's behavior is listed in the O section.

- D) Incorrect. Obvious information would have to be specifically stated and filed in the proper category.

30. A) **Correct.** Chakra energy channels function separately and together.
    B) Incorrect. There are seven chakras along the midline.
    C) Incorrect. Colors are an important aspect of chakra balancing.
    D) Incorrect. Body systems and functions are associated with chakras.

31. A) Incorrect. Approaching and accusing a coworker on one's own can have negative outcomes.
    B) Incorrect. If he is conscientious regarding ethical responsibilities, he should do something.
    C) Incorrect. The therapist has a strong suspicion but no actual proof.
    D) **Correct.** This is the best course of action and something management should address.

32. A) **Correct.** Ulcerative colitis may be considered an autoimmune disorder, but it is a chronic condition.
    B) Incorrect. Crohn's disease can affect any part of the gastrointestinal tract.
    C) Incorrect. Those who suffer from celiac disease experience intestinal inflammation when exposed to gluten, damaging and destroying intestinal villi and interfering with the digestion of nutrients.
    D) Incorrect. A goiter is an enlargement of the thyroid gland.

33. A) Incorrect. *Effleurage* is a French word that means to glide.
    B) Incorrect. Initial effleurage strokes allow the distribution of lotion.
    C) Incorrect. Effleurage strokes should sense muscle tone and tightness.
    D) **Correct.** Tapping and plucking are forms of tapotement.

34.
- **A) Correct.** A blood-borne pathogen lives in blood and can be transferred through bodily fluids.
- B) Incorrect. A blood-borne pathogen lives in human blood, not in plants.
- C) Incorrect. A blood-borne pathogen does not live in the air.
- D) Incorrect. Almost anything can carry germs; blood-borne pathogens are specifically microorganisms that cause disease and live in human blood.

35.
- **A) Correct.** Slow twitch fibers are related to muscle energy use; the term is not used in PNF.
- B) Incorrect. Spiral-diagonal is a primary tenet of PNF.
- C) Incorrect. Hold-relax is a type of PNF stretch.
- D) Incorrect. Contract-relax is a type of PNF stretch.

36.
- A) Incorrect. While these structures may contribute to the innate immune response, they are not formal structures of the immune system.
- B) Incorrect. Peyer's patches are located in the small intestine to monitor intestinal bacteria and tonsils are located in the throat, but neither are part of the functions of digestion.
- **C) Correct.** These are both secondary lymphatic structures.
- D) Incorrect. There is no relationship at all.

37.
- **A) Correct.** An intoxicated client can put a massage therapist's personal safety at risk.
- B) Incorrect. A contraindication is related to the assessment of a client's health.
- C) Incorrect. An intoxicated client does not necessarily have improper hygiene.
- D) Incorrect. A therapist should never massage a drunk client, regardless of the therapist's personal feelings about alcohol.

38.
- A) Incorrect. Polarity therapy was developed by osteopath Randolph Stone.
- B) Incorrect. Visceral manipulation was developed by an osteopath named Jean-Pierre Barral.
- C) Incorrect. Zero balancing was developed by an osteopath named Fritz Frederick Smith.
- **D) Correct.** Watsu was developed by Harold Dull, a practitioner of Zen shiatsu.

39.
- **A) Correct.** Everyone can benefit from massage.
- B) Incorrect. While babies do benefit from massage, they are not the only ones.
- C) Incorrect. Infant massage is an important practice.
- D) Incorrect. Elder massage is increasingly common.

40.
- **A) Correct.** Actin are thin filaments and myosin are thick filaments.
- B) Incorrect. Troponin and tropomyosin are protein molecules that cover actin filaments.
- C) Incorrect. ADP and phosphate molecules attach to myosin heads, and ATP results when ADP and phosphate molecules are energized.
- D) Incorrect. Epimysium is a connective tissue that surrounds a muscle and perimysium is a connective tissue that surrounds bundles of fascicles.

41.
- A) Incorrect. Cancer in the distant past does not imply the need for a doctor's clearance.
- **B) Correct.** If lymph nodes were removed, adapting a massage in a localized area may be necessary.
- C) Incorrect. This has nothing to do with a pre-massage assessment.
- D) Incorrect. This is a personal question and has nothing to do with a pre-massage assessment.

42.
- A) Incorrect. The client's actions would be listed in the O section.
- **B) Correct.** Any action or technique the therapist applied should be listed in the A section.

- C) Incorrect. New ideas should be listed in the *P* section.
- D) Incorrect. A recommendation for a new therapist should be listed in the *P* section.

43.
- A) Incorrect. The lower esophageal sphincter is located at the junction of the esophagus and the stomach.
- B) Incorrect. The sphincter of Oddi is located at the junction of the ileum and accessory organ ducts.
- C) Incorrect. The ileocecal sphincter is located at the junction of the small intestine and the colon.
- D) **Correct.** The pyloric sphincter is located at the junction of the stomach and small intestine.

44.
- A) Incorrect. Competence is an important aspect of providing a professional service.
- B) Incorrect. Honesty and integrity are qualities expected from a professional.
- C) **Correct.** Professional licensing does not hinge on status of membership in any particular organization.
- D) Incorrect. Maintaining client confidentiality is a professional requirement.

45.
- A) Incorrect. Airways relax in the sympathetic nervous system.
- B) **Correct.** Heart rate increases, airways relax, and epinephrine is secreted in the sympathetic nervous system.
- C) Incorrect. The bladder relaxes and digestion decreases in the sympathetic nervous system.
- D) Incorrect. Digestion decreases in the sympathetic nervous system.

46.
- A) Incorrect. Once lymph has been cleansed, lymphatic trunks route the fluid back to the venous bloodstream.
- B) Incorrect. The cisterna chyli does collect lymph draining from the abdomen and lower body.
- C) **Correct.** The vermiform appendix is a secondary lymphatic structure, but its modern purpose is not known.
- D) Incorrect. The spleen only receives lymph and stores platelets and lymphocytes.

47.
- A) Incorrect. SOAP notes are a clinical form of recordkeeping, not a laundry how-to list.
- B) Incorrect. SOAP notes are for individual clients.
- C) Incorrect. SOAP notes are to be kept in a client's file in the treatment office.
- D) **Correct.** SOAP notes track the progress of a client's pain and relief.

48.
- A) Incorrect. Saving time when a client has arrived late is not an excuse for failing to get informed consent.
- B) Incorrect. It does not matter how long a client has been seeing a therapist or the number of massages the client gets; informed consent must be obtained before each massage session begins.
- C) **Correct.** A massage therapist must always get informed consent before a massage.
- D) Incorrect. A client's deafness is not an excuse. A therapist must get informed consent using sign language, written discussion, establishing the client is a skilled lip-reader, or having a mutually agreed-upon interpreter in the room to assist with the exchange of dialogue.

49.
- A) Incorrect. In this case, the therapist has a moral and ethical responsibility to disclose.
- B) Incorrect. Abruptly ending a massage to call 911 can further affect the client's mental state at a time when he is clearly distraught.
- C) Incorrect. While this is something to do in the moment, it is not one's only obligation.
- D) **Correct.** Contacting an organization that is equipped to respond to public concerns and reports is the best option.

50.
- A) Incorrect. Synarthrotic joints are immovable.
- B) Incorrect. Diarthrotic joints move freely.
- C) Incorrect. Diarthrotic joints may be referred to as synovial joints.
- **D) Correct.** Amphiarthrotic joints are slightly movable.

51.
- A) Incorrect. Januvia® is an oral medication used to treat type 2 diabetes.
- B) Incorrect. Metformin is also used to treat type 2 diabetes.
- **C) Correct.** Prednisone may be used to treat allergic disorders, arthritis, blood disorders, breathing disorders, cancer, eye problems, immune system disorders, lupus, psoriasis, eye problems, and ulcerative colitis.
- D) Incorrect. Lisinopril is an ACE inhibitor that treats hypertension and congestive heart failure.

52.
- **A) Correct.** The goal of Reiki is to balance areas of the body where energy flow is either too strong or too weak, thus bringing the body into balance and enhancing its own healing ability.
- B) Incorrect. Craniosacral work is a light-touch method of assessing and enhancing the craniosacral system.
- C) Incorrect. Lomi lomi incorporates long, rhythmic, and fluid strokes using the hands and forearms.
- D) Incorrect. Raindrop technique uses essential oils applied in a sequence along the spine to reduce inflammation caused by viruses and bacteria.

53.
- A) Incorrect. This is false.
- B) Incorrect. While percussion helps to warm up muscles, it is not its main benefit.
- **C) Correct.** Percussion stimulates muscle firings.
- D) Incorrect. Nothing should be performed with harming a client in mind.

54.
- A) Incorrect. A massage therapist must have taken and passed courses and exams in order to practice professionally.
- **B) Correct.** A massage therapist must have taken and passed courses and exams in order to practice professionally.
- C) Incorrect. Even if licensed in another profession, an individual may not practice massage therapy without having passed courses and exams for licensure specifically in massage.
- D) Incorrect. Sports coaches may not legally practice massage without having passed certain courses and exams in order to be licensed therapists.

55.
- A) Incorrect. The digestive system responds innately using mechanical processing and chemical digestion.
- B) Incorrect. The integumentary system responds innately to invaders.
- **C) Correct.** The adaptive response by the lymphatic system is slow and highly selective.
- D) Incorrect. The respiratory system responds innately using cilia, sneezing, and coughing.

56.
- **A) Correct.** Transference may occur in a client-therapist relationship where there is a perceived imbalance of power.
- B) Incorrect. A dual relationship may involve a type of social relationship with a client outside of the client-therapist relationship, but it is not a psychological occurrence.
- C) Incorrect. A contraindication is a condition that affects the treatment plan of a massage therapist.
- D) Incorrect. A client continually attempting to engage with a therapist socially does not imply sexual misconduct.

57.
- A) Incorrect. The brain and spinal cord make up the central nervous system.
- B) Incorrect. These are the two distinct divisions of the nervous system.
- **C) Correct.** The parasympathetic relaxes and the sympathetic stimulates.

D) Incorrect. The somatic nervous system is part of the peripheral nervous system division and the brain is part of the central nervous system.

58.
A) Incorrect. Water represents winter, birth, and death.
B) Correct. Earth does represent late summer and nurturing.
C) Incorrect. Metal represents autumn and accumulation.
D) Incorrect. Wood represents spring and growth.

59.
A) Incorrect. A nonverbal cue may be an indicator of discomfort or relaxation.
B) Incorrect. Transference has no relationship to job titles.
C) Correct. A client's unconscious needs may trigger a therapist's unconscious needs.
D) Incorrect. Transference has nothing to do with workplace violations.

60.
A) Incorrect. Patient information should be listed on the intake form or in the S section.
B) Incorrect. Palliative care should be listed under the S section.
C) Correct. Future treatment plans and homework should be listed in the P section.
D) Incorrect. A performance review does not belong in the SOAP notes.

61.
A) Incorrect. This is the definition of a trigger point.
B) Incorrect. This is a definition of a latent trigger point.
C) Incorrect. Trigger points are also known as knots.
D) Correct. A trigger point is not necessarily near the tendon of a muscle.

62.
A) Incorrect. This is rude and gives the client the perception of an unprofessional environment.
B) Incorrect. This is unprofessional and disrespectful of personal boundaries.
C) Incorrect. The therapist should stay available while the client completes the intake form in case she has any questions.
D) Correct. This is professional and client centered.

63.
A) Incorrect. While a person should always exercise caution when crossing the street, this does not apply to professional safety for the massage therapist.
B) Incorrect. Exit routes should be clearly marked in the professional setting, but there is a better answer here.
C) Correct. Knowing what hazards and risks are present, and keeping them under control, is the definition of "being safe."
D) Incorrect. Identifying and addressing pain is to be done in treatment; it is not the same as "being safe."

64.
A) Incorrect. A synergist muscle assists movement.
B) Correct. The antagonist muscle opposes movement.
C) Incorrect. The prime mover is the main muscle in a movement and contracts the most.
D) Incorrect. A muscle acting as a fixator provides stability to a muscle movement.

65.
A) Incorrect. Shamans were believed to use magical abilities to get rid of illness and disease.
B) Incorrect. Shamans were viewed as healers who could fight off evil.
C) Correct. Shamans were respected and honored as healers.
D) Incorrect. A tribal shaman could be male or female.

66.
A) Incorrect. This is not hydrotherapy.
B) Incorrect. This is not hydrotherapy.
C) Correct. This is the correct definition of hydrotherapy.
D) Incorrect. This is not hydrotherapy.

67. A) Incorrect. The scapula articulates with the humerus forming the glenohumeral joint.
   B) Correct. The clavicle articulates with the manubrium forming the sternoclavicular joint.
   C) Incorrect. The scapula articulates with the clavicle forming the acromioclavicular joint.
   D) Incorrect. The hip articulates with the femur forming the acetabulofemoral joint.

68. A) Incorrect. Some medical conditions are contraindicated for massage that promotes circulation, but clients with these conditions may still benefit from a less intensive and noninvasive modality of massage.
   B) Correct. Pitted edema is a condition that is an absolute contraindication for massage.
   C) Incorrect. Someone who has a diagnosed aneurysm should not receive a Swedish massage.
   D) Incorrect. Someone in an acute state of an illness or injury should not receive a massage.

69. A) Incorrect. Petrissage is to knead.
   B) Correct. Effleurage strokes are performed at the beginning of the treatment.
   C) Incorrect. Friction occurs by working into the muscle belly to break up adhesions.
   D) Incorrect. Compressions involve stroking in a deep, rhythmic, and slow manner.

70. A) Incorrect. While repetitively shooting a gun could lead to trigger points, it is not a main development.
   B) Correct. Trigger points develop from injury and repetitive activity.
   C) Incorrect. This could be a definition of inflammation or varicose veins.
   D) Incorrect. This could be a cause of swollen limbs, varicose veins, or general soreness.

71. A) Incorrect. This may be good in the interim but it is not all the therapist should do.
   B) Incorrect. The therapist doesn't know if he informed his parents about what happened.
   C) Correct. This is the best course of action to assure that his parents know and that a state agency is aware.
   D) Incorrect. This action would most likely scare and upset the client.

72. A) Incorrect. The cortex is one of the two layers of the adrenal glands.
   B) Correct. The anterior lobe makes up 75 percent of the pituitary gland.
   C) Incorrect. The pituitary gland's posterior lobe stores and releases hormones produced by the hypothalamus.
   D) Incorrect. The medulla is one of the two layers of the adrenal glands.

73. A) Incorrect. Effleurage is to stroke gently.
   B) Incorrect. That is not the correct definition and might injure a client.
   C) Correct. Kneading is performed in circular, squeezing compressions in muscles and tendons.
   D) Incorrect. Squeezing the AC joint could harm the client.

74. A) Incorrect. Arteriosclerosis is a hardening of arteries and a reduction in arterial elasticity as the result of a buildup of calcium deposits.
   B) Correct. An aneurysm that ruptures causes hemorrhaging with a high risk of fatality.
   C) Incorrect. A hernia is a protrusion of an organ or other internal body material through the membrane that encases it.
   D) Incorrect. A decubitus ulcer, also referred to as a pressure ulcer or bedsore, is primarily the result of pressure preventing blood flow to an area.

75. A) Incorrect. These muscles are part of the abdominal group.

- **B)** **Correct.** Each column contains three muscles.
- C) Incorrect. These muscles assist with inhalation and exhalation.
- D) Incorrect. These muscles are involved in moving the mandible.

76.
- A) Incorrect. Vibrations, not percussion, shake the client.
- B) Incorrect. This definition is false.
- C) Incorrect. Though percussion may awaken a sleeping client, that is not its intention.
- **D)** **Correct.** Percussion, or tapotement, can help to loosen mucus and stimulate muscles.

77.
- A) Incorrect. A therapist may trade massages with another massage therapist, but that is an informal trade of one massage for another massage.
- **B)** **Correct.** Bartering is a commonly used way of exchanging services and is an accepted form of doing business under federal tax code.
- C) Incorrect. There is nothing inappropriate about bartering as long as services are fair and balanced and properly documented.
- D) Incorrect. Bartering is no riskier than an exchange of a service for a cash payment.

78.
- A) Incorrect. None of these terms is associated with reproduction.
- **B)** **Correct.** All of these terms are related to nervous system functions.
- C) Incorrect. None of these terms is associated with the urinary system.
- D) Incorrect. While the muscular system relies on the nervous system for movement, none of these terms is associated with the system.

79.
- A) Incorrect. Most illness begins during digestion is the core belief of Ayurveda.
- B) Incorrect. Practitioners of Ayurveda should create a healthy environment and avoid caustic ones.
- C) **Correct.** Ingestion of liquids and solids should be balanced.
- D) Incorrect. Adapting to seasonal changes is important.

80.
- A) Incorrect. Unless contraindicated by a doctor's note, a pregnant woman benefits from massage.
- B) Incorrect. Some pregnant women choose to have their massage therapist present to help them relax.
- C) Incorrect. Unless contraindicated by a doctor's note, a pregnant woman benefits from massage.
- **D)** **Correct.** If a pregnant woman is on bed rest under a doctor's care, it is best not to massage her.

81.
- A) Incorrect. Sports is a type of massage therapy.
- B) Incorrect. Lymphatic drainage is a type of massage therapy.
- **C)** **Correct.** Acrobatic is not a type of massage therapy.
- D) Incorrect. Swedish is a type of massage therapy.

82.
- A) Incorrect. Vibration is rapid, rhythmic, and maintains constant contact.
- B) Incorrect. Raking is a type of effleurage.
- **C)** **Correct.** Grasping and moving one hand clockwise and the other hand counterclockwise is a form of friction.
- D) Incorrect. Wringing is not a form of tapotement.

83.
- A) Incorrect. A therapist may end up jeopardizing the therapist-client relationship by bringing social interests into the massage room.
- B) Incorrect. A therapist may end up jeopardizing the therapist-client relationship by injecting herself into a client's social activities.
- **C)** **Correct.** Learning more about a therapist's involvement in and commitment to the practice of massage may help a client better appreciate the therapist's experience and professionalism; the client may even

refer other people to the therapist for massage.

D) Incorrect. Communicating negative information to a client about her sister's personal relationship will put the therapist in an awkward and unwelcome position.

84. **A)** **Correct.** A hydrocollator is a hot water tank filled with gel packs.

B) Incorrect. A hydrocollator is a water tank, but it is specifically used for hot therapy.

C) Incorrect. A hydrocollator is not a hot stone treatment.

D) Incorrect. A hydrocollator is not a cold therapy.

85. **A)** **Correct.** Alpha and beta cells are located in the pancreas and produce glucagon and insulin.

B) Incorrect. There is no relationship at all.

C) Incorrect. There is no relationship at all.

D) Incorrect. There is no relationship at all.

86. **A)** **Correct.** The stratum basale layer is the deepest of the five epidermis layers. It is also referred to as the stratum germinativum.

B) Incorrect. The stratum lucidum may not be present in all people or only in the hands and feet.

C) Incorrect. The stratum corneum only contains dead cells that flake off continuously.

D) Incorrect. The stratum spinosum is nicknamed the *prickly layer*.

87. A) Incorrect. HIV literally stands for *human immunodeficiency virus*.

B) **Correct.** Acne is a bacterial infection.

C) Incorrect. Herpes simplex is a virus that can be transmitted orally or sexually.

D) Incorrect. Clinically, shingles may be referred to as varicella zoster virus.

88. A) Incorrect. Herodicus is considered the father of sports medicine.

B) Incorrect. Johann Mezger is considered the founder of modern massage.

C) **Correct.** Hippocrates believed in observation, logical thought, and systematic principles of diagnosis.

D) Incorrect. Asclepius is known as the god of medicine and healing.

89. A) Incorrect. This is totally inappropriate and unethical.

B) Incorrect. The friend may not be aware of the confidentiality standards by which the therapist needs to abide.

C) Incorrect. There is no point in embarrassing or angering the client. Also, this response crosses boundaries.

D) **Correct.** This is the best answer. The therapist should state firmly and directly that he does not disclose personal information about a client.

90. **A)** **Correct.** Proximal-distal-proximal pumps blood out from the body, encouraging circulation throughout the limb, and then flushes it back toward the heart.

B) Incorrect. While working proximal-distal-proximal may help keep the therapist focused, that is not the reason to use this technique.

C) Incorrect. The client may not remain awake during treatment.

D) Incorrect. The principle does have meaning.

91. **A)** **Correct.** Cardiac muscle cells send out signals to begin the cardiac cycle. The sinoatrial node is the first to receive them.

B) Incorrect. The atrioventricular node receives the signals from the sinoatrial node.

C) Incorrect. The heart's conduction system has many components that keep the heart beating.

D) Incorrect. A sphygmomanometer is a device that measures blood pressure.

92. **A)** **Correct.** The sliding filament theory of muscle contraction is key to skeletal muscle movement.

- B) Incorrect. The musculoskeletal system works together but this theory is associated with the muscular system.
- C) Incorrect. There is a neuromuscular junction that creates a relationship between the muscular and nervous systems, but the sliding filament theory is related to muscle fiber movement.
- D) Incorrect. Smooth muscle does surround organs of digestion, but this theory is not related to the digestive process.

93.
- A) Incorrect. The proper working height can vary depending on the treatment, the therapist's comfort, and the size of the client.
- B) Incorrect. This is probably too high for a therapist to perform an effective treatment.
- C) **Correct.** The height depends on the therapist's comfort level when performing the massage.
- D) Incorrect. The height is dependent on what is comfortable for the therapist, not the client.

94.
- A) Incorrect. Mutual implies equal.
- B) Incorrect. In this relationship, the therapist has more power than the client does.
- C) Incorrect. While this is an agreement to provide a service for a fee, it is not how the role is defined.
- D) **Correct.** A client views the therapist as a professional with skills and knowledge that exceed her own.

95.
- A) **Correct.** Homeostasis means achieving balance in the body.
- B) Incorrect. Homeostasis means achieving balance in the body.
- C) Incorrect. Homeostasis means achieving balance in the body.
- D) Incorrect. Homeostasis means achieving balance in the body.

96.
- A) Incorrect. The biceps brachii is a fusiform muscle.
- B) Incorrect. The extensor digitorum longus is a unipennate muscle.
- C) Incorrect. The rectus abdominis is a parallel muscle.
- D) **Correct.** The pectoralis major is a convergent muscle.

97.
- A) Incorrect. This borders on diagnosis and implies the therapist can assure a remedy.
- B) **Correct.** If a client has had a pain for a long time, the therapist should inquire if she has seen a medical doctor to get an assessment of the condition.
- C) Incorrect. Drawing attention to a client's breast size and implying their size is the cause of chronic lower back pain is unprofessional.
- D) Incorrect. This may be an indication of a cause of lower back pain but this response sounds dismissive and condescending.

98.
- A) Incorrect. Bone growth is not directly affected by centripetal work.
- B) Incorrect. Metabolism is not directly affected by centripetal work.
- C) **Correct.** Working toward the heart helps to encourage blood flow back to the heart.
- D) Incorrect. Bladder contraction is not directly affected by centripetal work.

99.
- A) Incorrect. Sheets should be washed after each client.
- B) Incorrect. Sheets should never be used on more than one client.
- C) **Correct.** The rule is one set of sheets per one client.
- D) Incorrect. The sheets need to be changed and cleaned after each client.

100.
- A) **Correct.** Arterioles, capillaries, and venules are blood vessels in the circulatory system.
- B) Incorrect. While there are lymphatic capillaries, arterioles and venules are not vessels used in the lymphatic system.
- C) Incorrect. These terms are not associated with the integumentary system.
- D) Incorrect. These terms are not associated with the nervous system.

TWO: Practice Test Two

READ THE QUESTION CAREFULLY AND CHOOSE THE MOST CORRECT ANSWER.

1. Which is an example of a convergent muscle?
   A) biceps brachii
   B) extensor digitorum longus
   C) rectus abdominis
   D) pectoralis major

2. The exchange of gases between the blood and body tissues is referred to as what?
   A) internal respiration
   B) external respiration
   C) vital capacity
   D) pulmonary ventilation

3. A profession is defined as which of the following?
   A) an acceptable application of services
   B) a group of individuals who share the same occupation and perform the functions of the occupation in a consistent, moral, legal, and ethical manner
   C) a commitment to moral reasoning and character
   D) a code of conduct

4. Which of the following is NOT a contraindication for massage in a specific population?
   A) hypertension
   B) contagious disease
   C) open, infected surface wound
   D) general fatigue

5. Which of the following is NOT accurate about Avicenna?
   A) He was the first person in history who combined sports with medicine.
   B) He wrote about massage, exercise, and the value of hydrotherapies.
   C) He endorsed the use of friction techniques after athletic events.
   D) He valued touch and grooming in the care of horses.

6. How can therapists work most efficiently?
   A) use only their forearms
   B) call a friend to work with them
   C) use proper body mechanics
   D) quit

7. The first time a client comes to a therapist for a massage he complains about pain in his left shoulder he has had for six months. How should the therapist communicate when inquiring about this pain?
   A) "You should work on strengthening your upper body."
   B) "Oh, you probably have bilateral instability in your shoulder. I can fix that."
   C) "What did your doctor say when you discussed this with her?"
   D) "I bet you only sleep on your left side."

8. The endocrine system is made up of a group of what?
   A) gonads
   B) exocrine glands
   C) lymph nodes
   D) ductless glands

9. What type of massage is performed in small, circular movements, targeting deeper layers of muscles bound with adhesions or trigger points?
   A) effleurage massage
   B) friction massage
   C) cross-fiber friction massage
   D) lymphatic drainage massage

10. A general description of massage used by most United States agencies that regulate its practice usually includes a version of all the following but one. Which one?
    A) the manipulation and mobilization of soft tissue
    B) enhancement of muscle tone and circulation
    C) promotes relaxation
    D) physical therapy

11. Why should clients with hypertension NOT receive massage?
    A) Clients with hypertension are usually angry.
    B) Clients with hypertension have high blood pressure and massage can force movement of blood, leading to injury.
    C) Clients with hypertension are sensitive to touch.
    D) Clients with hypertension have high blood pressure and massage can cut off blood flow.

12. Which of the following is NOT one of OSHA's basic universal precautions?
    A) wearing sterile vinyl or latex gloves during treatment
    B) labeling and double-bagging contaminated waste
    C) washing hands after eating, drinking, or blowing one's nose
    D) wiping down massage equipment at the end of the day

13. The epiphyseal plate and periosteum are associated with which body system?
    A) reproductive
    B) skeletal
    C) muscular
    D) digestive

14. Which is a true statement?
    A) The left and right atrium are inferior to the left and right ventricle.
    B) The tricuspid valve is located between the right atrium and the right ventricle.
    C) The bicuspid valve is one of two semilunar valves.
    D) Semilunar valves connect the atrium chambers to their adjacent arteries.

15. Which is NOT true about the study of ethics?
    A) It is a relatively new field of study.
    B) It addresses rights and wrongs in societies.
    C) In helps to define rules of medical treatment and research.
    D) It looks at how discrimination affects group behavior.

16. An individual is seated on the floor with her legs extended. She extends her ankles until her toes point. Which term describes this action?
    A) dorsiflexion
    B) plantar flexion
    C) abduction
    D) eversion

17. What is NOT true about oocytes?
    A) Oocytes are immature eggs in females.
    B) An oocyte matures into an ovum inside an ovarian follicle.
    C) Oocytes are produced throughout a female's reproductive years.
    D) As females age, the quality and genetic stability of each oocyte begins to degrade.

18. Boundaries are most at risk of being crossed under which circumstance:
    A) when a client has come to a therapist exclusively for more than a year
    B) when a therapist goes to a client's home to perform a massage
    C) when a therapist works out of his home
    D) when the client is a coworker

19. Which of the following is NOT a type of skin cancer?
    A) cystic fibrosis
    B) basal cell carcinoma
    C) squamous cell carcinoma
    D) malignant melanoma

20. Which of the following is NOT true of a petrissage stroke?
    A) It is a superficial technique.
    B) It is a kneading technique that releases soft tissue.
    C) It may be referred to as *milking*.
    D) It involves lifting, squeezing, and rolling.

21. What is vasodilation?
    A) Blood vessels enlarge, increasing blood pressure.
    B) Blood vessels enlarge, decreasing blood pressure.
    C) Blood vessels dilate, increasing blood pressure.
    D) Blood vessels narrow, decreasing blood flow.

22. What is vasoconstriction?
    A) Blood vessels narrow, decreasing blood flow.
    B) Blood vessels expand, increasing blood flow.
    C) Blood vessels expand.
    D) Blood vessels narrow, increasing blood flow.

23. Which of the following should therapists NOT do to their nails?
    A) keep them short and filed
    B) keep them unpolished
    C) chew them short
    D) wash them regularly

24. A healthy client sees a massage therapist frequently, usually for a relaxation massage. When the client arrives for an appointment, she requests a deep tissue massage. What should the response be?

- **A)** "Oh, I really think we should stick with what is working."
- **B)** "No way. You will be in so much pain tomorrow."
- **C)** "Well, there is no reason why we cannot do that, but I do want you to be aware that you will most likely have some soreness in the next day or two. Are you comfortable with that?"
- **D)** "Why didn't you say so sooner? I could have been doing that all along."

25. Which of the following is NOT a sign of transference?

- **A)** overt adoration of the therapist
- **B)** lingering after the massage, keeping a therapist engaged in conversation
- **C)** asking for special considerations
- **D)** always leaving a big tip

26. Regarding traditional Chinese medicine's five steps, all of the following are true EXCEPT one. Which one?

- **A)** They are an assessment tool.
- **B)** They include observation of demeanor.
- **C)** They involve asking ten questions.
- **D)** They involve determining someone's dosha.

27. Therese C. Pfrimmer is credited with what type of massage modality?

- **A)** Esalen
- **B)** polarity therapy
- **C)** deep tissue
- **D)** visceral manipulation

28. What is the most appropriate stage of healing during which to apply cross-fiber treatment?

- **A)** acute
- **B)** subacute
- **C)** chronic
- **D)** pre-injury

29. Which of the following should therapists eat before going to work?

- **A)** a heavy, spicy meal
- **B)** nothing, to preserve hygiene
- **C)** a big, fibrous meal
- **D)** a balanced, nutritious meal

30. When signals travel down axons, what is it called?

- **A)** nerve impulse conduction
- **B)** saltatory
- **C)** continuous
- **D)** the reflex arc

31. In the lymphatic system, when a new invader is recognized by a t-cell, it communicates instructions to which cell?

- **A)** b-cell
- **B)** plasma cell
- **C)** memory cell
- **D)** an antibody-producing machine

32. How should a massage therapist treat a trigger point?

- **A)** effleurage, kneading, lymphatic draining, effleurage
- **B)** effleurage, kneading, friction, stretching, effleurage
- **C)** kneading, friction, kneading, effleurage
- **D)** effleurage, stretching, kneading, friction

33. George and Charles Taylor were brothers who are most noted for what?
    A). introducing Champissage to the United States
    B) bringing the Swedish massage cure to the United States
    C) inventing what is known today as Kellogg's Corn Flakes
    D) developing sports massage

34. Clients may refuse a massage when they arrive based on which of the following?
    A) The therapist is older or younger than expected.
    B) A client may refuse a massage without having to state why.
    C) The therapist is wearing a yarmulke.
    D) The therapist is wearing a wedding ring.

35. Which of the following is NOT true about pathology?
    A) The term is of Greek origin.
    B) It literally means the study of physiology.
    C) A pathologist studies how a disease progresses.
    D) It is an approach that determines the cause, development, effect on cells, and consequences of disease.

36. Which of the following is NOT true when performing strokes?
    A) Massage therapists should keep their hands relaxed, but firm.
    B) Massage therapists should bend their hands at a 45-degree angle.
    C) Massage therapists should keep their hands rigid and stiff.
    D) Massage therapists should hold their fingers together.

37. *Arrector pili* and *keloid* are terms most closely associated with which body system?
    A) endocrine
    B) integumentary
    C) respiratory
    D) muscular

38. Which meridian channel is paired with the heart?
    A) small intestine
    B) pericardium
    C) liver
    D) spleen

39. During a massage session, a client starts to passionately relay the horrible day she had at work. How should the massage therapist respond?
    A) "You think you had a bad day, let me tell you about mine."
    B) "Oh my gosh, I can't believe that happened!"
    C) "It seems like this massage came at a good time. It's great you have this chance to relax."
    D) "You really should be quiet! Your talking is probably disturbing other massages that are in session."

40. Which of the following statements is NOT true regarding thermotherapy?
    A) Short-term exposure to heat results in vasodilation.
    B) Someone with diabetes would greatly benefit from thermotherapy.
    C) Extended exposure to heat causes vasoconstriction.
    D) A hydrocollator may be used to heat packs filled with silicon.

41. Which of the following is NOT a type of tapotement/percussion?

- A) pincement
- B) clapping
- C) hacking
- D) kneading

42. Focusing attention on a client from arrival to departure is a sign of being what?

- A) aggressive
- B) client centered
- C) passive
- D) suspicious

43. According to the US Department of Labor's Occupational Outlook Handbook, 2016 – 17 Edition, what does a massage therapist NOT do?

- A) relieve pain
- B) improve circulation
- C) heal emotional scars
- D) relieve stress

44. An individual extends his arms horizontally and rotates them from the shoulders, making circles. Which term describes this action?

- A) circumduction
- B) pronation
- C) inversion
- D) rotation

45. What is the yang organ of digestion that peaks from 5 a.m. to 7 a.m.?

- A) lung
- B) stomach
- C) spleen
- D) large intestine

46. Which of the following muscles inserts on the greater trochanter?

- A) piriformis
- B) tensor fasciae latae
- C) biceps femoris
- D) psoas major

47. Chronic obstructive pulmonary disease (COPD) is a collection of chronic lung conditions. Which of the following is NOT considered part of COPD?

- A) asthma
- B) bronchitis
- C) emphysema
- D) migraine

48. Which statement is most correct regarding what happened after the fall of the Roman Empire?

- A) Medical education was spread across the globe.
- B) Hydrotherapy became a treatment enjoyed by all instead of just soldiers and the wealthy citizens of Rome.
- C) Massage and touch were important for the care of the sick and dying.
- D) Women were denied the right to provide care to those who were sick and dying.

49. If a client tells a therapist he was doing a job in someone's home and stole a credit card he saw on a desk, the therapist should do what?

- A) ask the client to buy her lunch
- B) tell the client the therapist did the same thing once and never got caught
- C) contact the police
- D) avoid responding as it's none of her business

50. How can therapists produce more force in their treatment?
- **A)** push harder on the client
- **B)** keep their back foot grounded and use a fist or elbow
- **C)** use their feet
- **D)** punch the client

51. Oocytes and gametes are associated with which body system?
- **A)** immune
- **B)** integumentary
- **C)** reproductive
- **D)** respiratory

52. Smell, taste, vision, and hearing are related to what kind of sense?
- **A)** afferent
- **B)** efferent
- **C)** special
- **D)** Wernicke's

53. What is a benefit of effleurage?
- **A)** releasing trigger points
- **B)** warming up the tissue with long, fluid strokes
- **C)** high stress
- **D)** spreading muscle fibers with deep, squeezing strokes

54. What type of treatment uses water in any of its forms to achieve therapeutic benefits?
- **A)** effleurage
- **B)** hydrotherapy
- **C)** hot stone
- **D)** ice massage

55. Sexually fantasizing about a client may be a sign of what?
- **A)** countertransference
- **B)** sexual misconduct
- **C)** unethical workplace behavior
- **D)** client-centeredness

56. What does the prefix *brady–* refer to?
- **A)** small
- **B)** slow
- **C)** vessels
- **D)** the lungs

57. Which of the following is a classification of a boundary related to massage?
- **A)** competence
- **B)** character
- **C)** education
- **D)** personal

58. Which of the following best describes the relationship between the federal government and massage?
- **A)** The federal government regulates massage licensing requirements.
- **B)** The federal government provides grants and loans.
- **C)** The federal government requires all massage therapists to take HIV/AIDS courses.
- **D)** The federal government oversees the content of all massage licensing exams.

59. Which meridian channel terminates in front of the ear at the temporomandibular joint?
- **A)** heart
- **B)** large intestine
- **C)** small intestine
- **D)** kidney

60. Skeletal bones go through a remodeling process throughout the lifetime. What role do osteoclasts play in this process?
    A) They form new bone.
    B) They become embedded in the bone matrix.
    C) They break down bone.
    D) They signal to the endocrine system to release calcitonin.

61. What role does the pancreas play in the digestive system?
    A) It produces bile.
    B) It stores bile.
    C) It produces an enzymatic juice that breaks down carbohydrates, fats, and proteins.
    D) None. It is an organ of the endocrine system.

62. A client who regularly sees a massage therapist always leaves a tip significantly below average. The therapist finds she is adding a few more minutes to each massage and making exceptions to her schedule to accommodate the client, hoping the tip will improve. What might this indicate?
    A) transference
    B) poor massage technique
    C) countertransference
    D) a struggling client who just cannot afford a better tip

63. What is the best way to ensure a good tax year, without an audit?
    A) paying a bookie to wipe one's record clean
    B) moving to Canada
    C) having a family member in the IRS
    D) proper bookkeeping with incomes and expenses listed clearly

64. What is an embolism?
    A) a thickening of arterial walls
    B) a pain in the chest resulting from insufficient blood flow to the heart
    C) a blood clot or gas bubble
    D) when spinal disk material protrudes beyond the vertebrae

65. What is a contraindication for using hot therapy?
    A) spastic muscles
    B) trigger points
    C) hypertension
    D) bound fascia

66. What does the word root *opia* refer to?
    A) sight
    B) breathing
    C) kidneys
    D) pain

67. Which part of the small intestine is where most of the nutrients are absorbed?
    A) ileum
    B) jejunum
    C) duodenum
    D) cecum

68. What is the value of using a self-assessment technique?
    A) It is a good way to determine if rates should be increased.
    B) It is a good way to prepare for a meeting with a supervisor.
    C) It is a good way to analyze a moment during a massage that blurred a boundary.
    D) It is a good tool for assessing if new staff should be added.

69. What is a contraindication for using cold therapy?
  A) returning the body to homeostasis
  B) reducing pain
  C) decreasing inflammation
  D) Reynaud's disease

70. What does the acronym *RICE* stand for?
  A) Rest, Ice, Compression, Elevation
  B) Rest Instantly, Constantly Evaluate
  C) Rest, Injure, Contact, Emergency
  D) Run, Ice, Cold, Exercise

71. If a regular client states to a therapist, "my cancer has returned," what should the therapist do?
  A) Make an excuse to step out of the room so the client does not see the therapist crying.
  B) Inform the client it is unlikely that the massages have triggered the return of the cancer.
  C) Empathetically and delicately share with the client that professionally a massage is not recommended without medical clearance.
  D) Use the massage time to provide emotional support and comfort.

72. Which of the following statements is NOT correct about proprioceptors?
  A) Proprioceptors are only found in muscles.
  B) They are important in muscle memory and hand-eye coordination.
  C) Muscle spindles and Golgi tendon organs are two types of proprioceptors.
  D) They communicate speed, angles, and balance to the central nervous system.

73. Which of the following is NOT required for independent contractors?
  A) filing a W-2
  B) filing a W-9
  C) saving a percentage of each paycheck
  D) filing their own taxes

74. Which of the following terms is NOT related to the sliding filament theory of muscle contraction?
  A) cross bridge
  B) recovery stroke
  C) vasodilation
  D) action potential

75. When clients show up for a scheduled appointment, they are giving what?
  A) implied consent to perform massage
  B) voluntary consent to perform massage
  C) informed consent to perform massage
  D) absolute consent to perform massage

76. Which of the following cannot be used as a tool during massage?
  A) elbow
  B) thumb
  C) forearm
  D) ninja star

77. What is the common name for eponychium?
  A) a hair strand
  B) fingernail
  C) cuticle
  D) hair follicle

78. What should therapists NOT bring to a job interview?
- A) a good work ethic
- B) a wrinkly outfit
- C) their resume
- D) their license

79. The concept of the energy body has its roots in which type of medicine?
- A) Western
- B) allopathic
- C) Eastern
- D) complementary and alternative

80. What is the name of the lid-like piece of cartilage that covers the trachea?
- A) alveoli
- B) epiglottis
- C) hyaline cartilage
- D) bronchi

81. What is sports massage?
- A) a game that is played for therapeutic benefits
- B) a technique that helps athletes perform to their best ability
- C) deep compressions along bony ridges
- D) light strokes to encourage lymph flow

82. Which of the following is NOT an example of a reprimand in the workplace?
- A) a letter from the board in the state in which the therapist practices
- B) verbal
- C) written
- D) immediate termination

83. Which meridian channel is considered the root of life and stores essence?
- A) heart
- B) gallbladder
- C) kidney
- D) liver

84. What is NOT an effect of effleurage?
- A) pliable tissue
- B) increased blood flow
- C) high levels of stress
- D) relaxation

85. In what population does the hormone relaxin release its highest levels?
- A) babies
- B) the elderly
- C) pregnant women
- D) teenagers

86. The horizontal plane of the body is also referred to as which of the following?
- A) midsagittal
- B) coronal
- C) transverse
- D) sagittal

87. Employers have the right to expect their employees to do all of the following EXCEPT
- A) refrain from lewd and foul language in the workplace.
- B) dress in clean, modest, and professional attire.
- C) perform massages free of charge on days the employer is fundraising for a local charity.
- D) refrain from negative talk about coworkers.

88. Which of the following would NOT be considered a massage business workplace violation?

   A) using a company computer without permission
   B) using the onsite washing machine and dryer to do personal laundry
   C) refusing to stay after hours to massage a walk-in client
   D) gathering client information for a side business unrelated to massage

89. Why do massage therapists need insurance?

   A) Accidents happen, but risk can be avoided.
   B) People are terrible and looking to make money.
   C) Without liability insurance, they have to pay taxes.
   D) They want to sue their clients.

90. Which of the following best describes a type of bony landmark referred to as a ramus?

   A) It is formed by two diverging lines.
   B) It is a prominent elevation.
   C) It is an opening or canal.
   D) It is an arm or branch of a bone.

91. Which of the following statements is NOT true?

   A) There are twelve cranial nerves.
   B) There are twenty-four vertebrae in a human adult's vertebral column.
   C) There are ten pairs of ribs.
   D) There are twenty-six bones in a human foot.

92. Which of the following drugs is potentially addictive?

   A) Crestor®
   B) Vyvanse®
   C) Lyrica®
   D) Coumadin®

93. Which of the following best describes a type of bony landmark referred to as a foramen?

   A) It is a bulge.
   B) It guides and limits motion.
   C) It is a hole in a bone for nerves or vessels to pass through.
   D) It is a narrow, slender projection.

94. What is NOT a benefit of lymphatic drainage massage?

   A) It reduces swelling and edema.
   B) It assists in surgery recovery.
   C) It releases trigger points.
   D) It increases energy.

95. Which may be the repercussion of an employee talking about a really obese client in the break room of a place of business?

   A) None. It is okay as long as the conversation is with a coworker the therapist is friends with outside of work.
   B) Management informs the therapist he will no longer be allowed to massage that client.
   C) The therapist may receive a written warning of termination by his employer.
   D) The therapist tells the staff member who schedules the appointments he will buy her dinner if she does not schedule the therapist with that client again.

96. What is the purpose of a business plan?

- **A)** to show the best way to make the most money
- **B)** to beg investors for money
- **C)** to clearly outline realistic business goals
- **D)** to show clients that the therapist is a serious professional

97. The pectineus is part of which muscle group?

- **A)** lateral rotators
- **B)** quadriceps femoris
- **C)** hamstring
- **D)** adductor

98. In traditional Chinese medicine's five elements theory, what nourishes wood?

- **A)** earth
- **B)** water
- **C)** metal
- **D)** fire

99. What is proprioception?

- **A)** the ability to sense one's body in relation to space
- **B)** the ability to move better
- **C)** the ability to become aware of something through the senses
- **D)** the ability to sense pain

100. Which of the following bones is roughly shaped like a cube and, generally, is as wide as it is long?

- **A)** irregular
- **B)** sesamoid
- **C)** short
- **D)** long

PRACTICE TEST TWO ANSWER KEY

1.
   A) Incorrect. The biceps brachii is a fusiform muscle.
   B) Incorrect. The extensor digitorum longus is a unipennate muscle.
   C) Incorrect. The rectus abdominis is a parallel muscle.
   D) Correct. The pectoralis major is a convergent muscle.

2.
   A) Correct. Internal respiration is the exchange of gases between the blood and body tissues.
   B) Incorrect. External respiration occurs between the alveoli and blood capillaries.
   C) Incorrect. Vital capacity refers to the greatest volume of air that can be pulled into the lungs.
   D) Incorrect. Pulmonary ventilation relates to inspiration and expiration.

3.
   A) Incorrect. A code of ethics describes an acceptable application of services.
   B) Correct. Massage therapists, accountants, and psychologists each make up groups of people that are examples of professions.
   C) Incorrect. Moral reasoning and character are part of ethical behavior.
   D) Incorrect. A code of conduct is a written statement of guiding principles and expectations related to day-to-day responsibilities, procedures, and professional conduct, as well as the repercussions of infractions.

4.
   A) Incorrect. Hypertension may often contraindicate work.
   B) Incorrect. A contagious disease may often contraindicate work.
   C) Incorrect. An open and infected surface wound may often contraindicate work.
   D) Correct. General fatigue is not a contraindication to receiving work.

5.
   A) Correct. Herodicus, a fifth-century BCE Greek doctor, was the first known historical medical figure to link sports with medicine.
   B) Incorrect. Avicenna did write about massage, exercise, and the value of hydrotherapies.
   C) Incorrect. Avicenna did endorse the use of friction techniques.
   D) Incorrect. Avicenna believed valued horses benefited from touch and grooming after physical activity.

6.
   A) Incorrect. Using only forearms can lead to issues for both the therapist and the client.
   B) Incorrect. Unless providing a specific treatment that calls for two therapists, a massage therapist is an independent worker and should not need a partner during treatment.
   C) Correct. Proper body mechanics allow a therapist to work efficiently without working hard.
   D) Incorrect. Quitting is not a good work practice!

7.
   A) Incorrect. Drawing attention to a client's physique is unprofessional.
   B) Incorrect. This borders on diagnosis and implies the therapist can assure a remedy.
   C) Correct. If a client has had a pain for a long time, the therapist should inquire if he has seen a medical doctor to get an assessment of the condition.
   D) Incorrect. This may be an indication of a cause of shoulder pain but this response sounds dismissive and condescending.

8.
   A) Incorrect. Gonads are found in the reproductive system.
   B) Incorrect. Exocrine glands have ducts and do not feed directly into the bloodstream.
   C) Incorrect. Lymph nodes are found in the lymphatic system.
   D) Correct. Ductless glands secrete hormones in the endocrine system.

9. A) Incorrect. Effleurage strokes are long and fluid, warming up tissue and promoting relaxation.
    B) Incorrect. Friction massage uses the therapist's digits to work into adhesions in the direction of muscle fibers.
    C) **Correct.** Cross-fiber friction uses superficial layers to work out adhesions in deeper layers of tissue.
    D) Incorrect. Lymphatic drainage massage is very light work that pumps and moves lymph flow.

10. A) Incorrect. Skin, fascia, tendons, ligaments, and muscles are classified as soft tissue.
    B) Incorrect. Massage is considered to enhance muscle tone and circulation.
    C) Incorrect. Massage is believed to promote relaxation.
    D) **Correct.** In the United States, physical therapy is usually viewed as a separate profession.

11. A) Incorrect. Clients with hypertension aren't necessarily angry people.
    B) **Correct.** Massage can increase blood flow when blood vessels are already pressed to their limit, and this could lead to harm for the client.
    C) Incorrect. Clients with hypertension are not necessarily supersensitive.
    D) Incorrect. Massage does not cut off blood flow.

12. A) Incorrect. Wearing gloves during treatment can help prevent the spread of disease.
    B) Incorrect. Labeling and double-bagging contaminated waste is a basic precaution.
    C) Incorrect. Washing hands is a great way to prevent disease from spreading.
    D) **Correct.** Equipment should be wiped down after each massage treatment, between clients.

13. A) Incorrect. There is no relationship at all.
    B) **Correct.** The periosteum is a connective tissue used to build and maintain bones and the epiphyseal plate is the growth place on long bone.
    C) Incorrect. There is no relationship at all.
    D) Incorrect. There is no relationship at all.

14. A) Incorrect. The left and right atrium are *superior* to the left and right ventricle.
    B) **Correct.** The tricuspid valve is one of two atrioventricular valves.
    C) Incorrect. The bicuspid valve is one of two atrioventricular valves.
    D) Incorrect. Semilunar valves connect the *ventricle* chambers to their adjacent arteries.

15. A) **Correct.** The study of ethics extends back thousands of years.
    B) Incorrect. The core of ethics is establishing what is morally right and wrong.
    C) Incorrect. The practice of medicine and medical research are guided by ethics.
    D) Incorrect. Discrimination against an individual or groups of individuals is an ethical concern.

16. A) Incorrect. Dorsiflexion is a flexion of the foot in which the toes face upward towards the ceiling.
    B) Correct. Plantar flexion is an extension of the ankle.
    C) Incorrect. Abduction is movement away from the body, such as moving the arms to a horizontal position.
    D) Incorrect. Eversion is the elevation of the lateral edge of the foot.

17. A) Incorrect. Females are born with oocytes.
    B) Incorrect. Every month several oocytes may mature into ovum but only one is released.
    C) **Correct.** What a female is born with is her only supply.
    D) Incorrect. As a female ages, the possibility of pregnancy lessens.

18. A) **Correct.** The longer a massage therapist has been massaging a client, the higher the risk of boundaries

		becoming blurred and crossed due to the strong and trusting relationship between the two individuals.
	B)	Incorrect. A massage therapist working in someone's home will likely be more protective of boundaries.
	C)	Incorrect. A massage therapist who practices at home should be more alert regarding boundaries.
	D)	Incorrect. A massage should always be conducted professionally and within boundaries, regardless of the relationship with the client.
19.	**A)**	**Correct.** Cystic fibrosis is a genetic disorder.
	B)	Incorrect. Basal cell carcinoma is a type of skin cancer.
	C)	Incorrect. Squamous cell carcinoma is a form of skin cancer.
	D)	Incorrect. Malignant melanoma is a type of skin cancer.
20.	**A)**	**Correct.** It is a technique that usually follows effleurage and is deeper and more aggressive than effleurage.
	B)	Incorrect. *Petrissage* is a French term that refers to kneading.
	C)	Incorrect. *Petrissage* may be referred to as a milking technique.
	D)	Incorrect. *Petrissage* does involve lifting, squeezing, and rolling of the skin and underlying fascia.
21.	A)	Incorrect. This would be cause for concern.
	B)	**Correct.** In vasodilation, blood vessels widen, allowing blood more room to travel and thus lessening pressure.
	C)	Incorrect. This is the same as answer A.
	D)	Incorrect. This is vasoconstriction.
22.	**A)**	**Correct.** Vasoconstriction occurs when the blood vessel walls narrow, giving blood less room to travel, thus increasing its pressure.
	B)	Incorrect. This is vasodilation.
	C)	Incorrect. This is part of vasodilation.
	D)	Incorrect. This is not a condition.

23.	A)	Incorrect. A therapist's nails should be short and filed.
	B)	Incorrect. A therapist's nails should be unpolished.
	C)	**Correct.** Therapists should not chew their nails.
	D)	Incorrect. Therapists should wash their hands and nails regularly.
24.	A)	Incorrect. The client has the right to request a different kind of massage. Implying the therapist knows better when the client has no contraindications for deep tissue massage is not advisable.
	B)	Incorrect. This is a condescending and dismissive response.
	C)	**Correct.** In this case, the therapist should remain open to the client's request while informing her of potential outcomes and side effects; this allows the client to make an informed and voluntary decision.
	D)	Incorrect. This response sounds aggressive and may offend or embarrass the client.
25.	A)	Incorrect. Overt adoration of the therapist and her or his skills can suggest transference.
	B)	Incorrect. Not being able to disconnect from the therapist after the service is complete can suggest transference.
	C)	Incorrect. Wanting special treatment from a therapist may suggest transference.
	D)	**Correct.** Showing financial appreciation for a therapist's work is not a sign of transference.
26.	A)	Incorrect. The five steps are used as an assessment tool.
	B)	Incorrect. Observation of demeanor is one of the five steps.
	C)	Incorrect. Described as the ten questions, it is one of the five steps.
	D)	**Correct.** Doshas are related to Ayurveda.

27. A) Incorrect. Esalen massage was developed in the 1960s at the Esalen Institute in Big Sur, CA.

B) Incorrect. Polarity therapy was developed by Dr. Randolph Stone.

C) Correct. Therese C. Pfrimmer is credited with developing deep tissue techniques. Her Pfrimmer Deep Muscle Therapy is still taught today.

D) Incorrect. Visceral manipulation was developed by an osteopath named Jean-Pierre Barral.

28. A) Incorrect. The tissue is still repairing in the acute stage. Vigorous treatment could further damage it.

B) Correct. The initial healing process is complete and the adhesions are still forming, allowing the perfect, pliable window to start treatment.

C) Incorrect. While therapists can perform cross-fiber treatment in chronic stages, it is best to start the treatment earlier in the healing process.

D) Incorrect. This is not a stage of healing.

29. A) Incorrect. A heavy meal can slow down a therapist and make him sleepy.

B) Incorrect. Therapists should eat something before their shifts so they have energy. A small, nutritious meal will not interfere with personal hygiene.

C) Incorrect. A big meal with lots of fiber can produce negative effects in a small treatment room.

D) Correct. A therapist should eat a filling, nutritious meal that gives her energy to work.

30. **A) Correct.** Nerve impulses are conducted down myelinated and unmyelinated axons.

B) Incorrect. The term *saltatory* means a nerve conduction down a myelinated axon.

C) Incorrect. The term *continuous* means a nerve conduction down an unmyelinated axon.

D) Incorrect. The reflex arc is a neural pathway that controls the reflex response.

31. **A) Correct.** B-cells receive instructions from t-cells.

B) Incorrect. B-cells mature into plasma cells.

C) Incorrect. A memory cell recognizes a specific invading organism immediately.

D) Incorrect. Plasma cells may informally be referred to as *antibody-producing machines*.

32. A) Incorrect. This treatment may aggravate a trigger point more.

B) Correct. This treatment includes warming up the tissue, working deeply to release the trigger point, stretching the taut muscle, and easing out of the tissue.

C) Incorrect. This treatment may aggravate a trigger point more.

D) Incorrect. This treatment may aggravate a trigger point more.

33. A) Incorrect. Champissage is a type of scalp massage that was derived from the Ayurvedic *champi*, meaning head massage.

B) Correct. After studying the Swedish massage cure in Europe, they returned to the United States to practice and published the first textbook on the subject.

C) Incorrect. John Harvey Kellogg and his brother co-invented what we know today as Kellogg's Corn Flakes.

D) Incorrect. Jack Meager is considered the pioneer of sports massage.

34. A) Incorrect. A client may not refuse a massage based on the therapist's age. Furthermore, a business cannot accept age discrimination as a reason not to charge a client who arrives for a scheduled massage.

B) Correct. Clients are not required to disclose why they decided to cancel the massage after they met the therapist.

- C) Incorrect. A client may not refuse a massage based on the therapist's religion. Furthermore, a business cannot accept religious discrimination as a reason not to charge a client who arrives for a scheduled massage.
- D) Incorrect. A client may not refuse a massage based on the therapist's marital status. Furthermore, a business cannot accept marital status of a therapist as a reason not to charge a client who arrives for a scheduled massage.

35.
- A) Incorrect. Pathology is a Greek term.
- **B) Correct.** Pathology literally means the study of disease, not physiology.
- C) Incorrect. A pathologist does study the progression of a disease.
- D) Incorrect. Pathology is an approach that strives to determine the cause, development, the effect on cells, and consequences of a disease.

36.
- A) Incorrect. The therapist's hands should be relaxed and firm.
- B) Incorrect. As long as the therapist's wrists are not bent at a 90-degree angle, this is fine.
- **C) Correct.** Therapists' hands should not be rigid and stiff.
- D) Incorrect. The therapist's fingers should stay together to perform fluid strokes.

37.
- A) Incorrect. There is no relationship at all.
- **B) Correct.** Arrector pili are small muscles that hold hair follicles in place and keloid is a type of scar formed on the skin.
- C) Incorrect. There is no relationship at all.
- D) Incorrect. While arrector pili are muscles, they only serve a purpose in the integumentary system.

38.
- **A) Correct.** The heart is a yin organ and the small intestine is a yang organ.
- B) Incorrect. The pericardium is paired with the triple warmer.
- C) Incorrect. The liver is paired with the gallbladder.
- D) Incorrect. The spleen is paired with the stomach.

39.
- A) Incorrect. This response moves the session away from being client-centered and opens the door to crossing boundaries.
- B) Incorrect. This response sounds like it is encouraging the client to keep talking.
- **C) Correct.** This response is client centered and also a polite hint to the client to refocus on the intent of the session.
- D) Incorrect. This is an overly aggressive and rude response.

40.
- A) Incorrect. Short-term exposure to heat results in vasodilation, which increases blood flow.
- **B) Correct.** Someone with diabetes may have a problem sensing temperature variations.
- C) Incorrect. Extended exposure to heat causes vasoconstriction and perspiration in order to return the body to a state of homeostasis.
- D) Incorrect. A hydrocollator contains heated water in which packs are immersed to heat. They are most commonly used in chiropractic offices and physical therapy clinics.

41.
- A) Incorrect. Pincement is a light type of tapotement/percussion.
- B) Incorrect. Clapping is a heavy type of tapotement/percussion.
- C) Incorrect. Hacking is a heavy type of tapotement/percussion.
- **D) Correct.** Kneading is not a type of tapotement/percussion.

42.
- A) Incorrect. Aggressive behavior is intimidating and overbearing.
- **B) Correct.** Being client centered is an important role for a massage therapist.
- C) Incorrect. Being passive with a client may result in the therapist being taken advantage of or boundaries to be crossed.

	D)	Incorrect. Being attentive to paying clients does not suggest a therapist is suspicious of them.
43.	A)	Incorrect. It states, "With their touch, therapists relieve pain."
	B)	Incorrect. It states, "With their touch, therapists . . . improve circulation."
	C)	**Correct.** Healing emotional scars is not included in the handbook.
	D)	Incorrect. It states, "With their touch, therapists . . . relieve stress."
44.	A)	Correct. In circumduction, circular movement occurs distally while the joint stays fixed.
	B)	Incorrect. Pronation is medial rotation of the forearm.
	C)	Incorrect. Inversion is the elevation of the medial edge of the foot.
	D)	Incorrect. Unlike circumduction, rotation is not a complete circle.
45.	A)	Incorrect. The lung is a yin organ of circulation that peaks from 3 a.m. to 5 a.m.
	B)	Incorrect. The stomach is a yang organ of digestion that peaks from 7 a.m. to 9 a.m.
	C)	Incorrect. The spleen is a yin organ of circulation that peaks from 9 a.m. to 11 a.m.
	D)	**Correct.** The large intestine is a yang organ of digestion that peaks from 5 a.m. to 7 a.m.
46.	**A)**	**Correct.** The piriformis is a lateral rotator of the hip and inserts on the greater trochanter.
	B)	Incorrect. The tensor fasciae latae inserts on the iliotibial tract.
	C)	Incorrect. The biceps femoris inserts on the head of the fibula.
	D)	Incorrect. The psoas major inserts on the lesser trochanter.
47.	A)	Incorrect. An asthma attack causes coughing, wheezing, and difficulty breathing.
	B)	Incorrect. Bronchitis occurs when the bronchial tubes are inflamed and mucus production increases.
	C)	Incorrect. Emphysema occurs when the alveoli in the lungs are severely damaged or destroyed.
	D)	**Correct.** A migraine occurs when cranial blood vessels dilate.
48.	A)	Incorrect. After the fall of the Roman Empire, medical knowledge was not widely valued in Europe.
	B)	Incorrect. Baths were viewed as glorification of the body and were banned.
	C)	**Correct.** The concept of massage and touch was viewed as valuable to the Christian rituals of care for the sick and dying.
	D)	Incorrect. Women were primarily responsible for care under the authority of the church.
49.	A)	Incorrect. This response is unethical.
	B)	Incorrect. This disclosure is unethical and indicates societal misbehavior.
	C)	**Correct.** A client disclosed a crime and the therapist has a legal obligation to report to the police knowledge of a crime.
	D)	Incorrect. Not responding to the client's disclosure during the massage is fine, but does not mean the therapist should not report the crime.
50.	A)	Incorrect. Pushing into a client is not pleasant for the client or the therapist.
	B)	**Correct.** In order to produce more force, tools like the fist or elbow can be used, while the therapist grounds more in the back foot.
	C)	Incorrect. It is not common to use feet in a standard table treatment.
	D)	Incorrect. Punching the client is always unacceptable.
51.	A)	Incorrect. There is no relationship at all.
	B)	Incorrect. There is no relationship at all.
	C)	**Correct.** Oocytes are immature eggs and gametes are eggs and sperm.

D) Incorrect. There is no relationship at all.

52. A) Incorrect. An afferent nerve sends information to the brain.
    B) Incorrect. An efferent nerve receives motor signals from the brain.
    C) Correct. The special senses perceive stimuli from the external environment through smell, taste, vision, and hearing.
    D) Incorrect. The Wernicke's area is a part of the temporal lobe important for recognizing speech and interpreting words.

53. A) Incorrect. Trigger point release is deeper work that comes after effleurage strokes.
    B) Correct. Effleurage warms up tissue with long, fluid strokes.
    C) Incorrect. Effleurage should produce decreased stress.
    D) Incorrect. Compression spreads muscle fibers with deep, squeezing strokes.

54. A) Incorrect. Effleurage does not use water, specifically.
    B) Correct. Hydrotherapy is a treatment that uses water in any of its forms to achieve therapeutic benefits.
    C) Incorrect. Hot stone massage does not use water, specifically.
    D) Incorrect. Ice massage is a type of hydrotherapy, but it only uses one form of water.

55. **A) Correct.** Fantasizing about a client is one of the signs of countertransference.
    B) Incorrect. If no action beyond the fantasy is taken, it is not sexual misconduct.
    C) Incorrect. It is not unethical workplace behavior unless the therapist discusses this fantasy with the client or a coworker or physically acts upon it.
    D) Incorrect. Client-centeredness is focusing on the client in a professional manner.

56. A) Incorrect. The prefix *micro–* means small, as in microorganism.
    B) Correct. The prefix *brady–* means slow, as in bradycardia, a slow pulse rate.
    C) Incorrect. The prefix *angio–* refers to vessels. For instance, an angioplasty is a procedure that widens obstructed arteries or veins.
    D) Incorrect. The prefix *pulmo–* refers to the lungs. For example, the pulmonary artery moves de-oxygenated blood from the heart to the lungs.

57. A) Incorrect. Working competently is part of scope of practice.
    B) Incorrect. Someone's character can be good, bad, or questionable, but is not a boundary.
    C) Incorrect. Education may factor in to intellectual boundaries, but it is not a boundary itself.
    D) Correct. Personal boundaries are formed by an individual's upbringing, his or her own beliefs and comfort levels, and his or her life circumstances.

58. A) Incorrect. Individual states regulate massage licensing requirements.
    B) Correct. The federal government provides grants and loans to massage students.
    C) Incorrect. Individual states determine if HIV/AIDS courses are required.
    D) Incorrect. The federal government has no oversight of massage licensing exams.

59. A) Incorrect. The heart meridian channel terminates on the radial side of the little finger.
    B) Incorrect. The large intestine meridian channel crosses underneath the nose and terminates on the other side of the midline.
    C) Correct. The small intestine meridian channel terminates in front of the ear at the TMJ.
    D) Incorrect. The kidney meridian channel terminates at the clavicle.

60. A) Incorrect. Osteoblasts form new bone.
B) Incorrect. Osteoblasts get embedded in bone matrix and then become identified as osteocytes.
C) Correct. Osteoclasts break down bone for remodeling.
D) Incorrect. It is calcitonin that signals to the osteoclasts to begin breaking down bone.

61. A) Incorrect. The liver produces bile.
B) Incorrect. The gallbladder stores bile.
C) Correct. The enzymatic juice produced by the pancreas is delivered to the duodenum.
D) Incorrect. The pancreas is used by both the digestive and endocrine systems.

62. A) Incorrect. Transference is a behavior directed from the client onto the therapist.
B) Incorrect. If the therapist's other clients leave average or above-average tips, then this is not the issue.
C) Correct. The therapist is personalizing the situation too much by assuming she is doing something wrong.
D) Incorrect. If the client can afford to see a massage therapist regularly and pay for the session, then the client can afford a better tip.

63. A) Incorrect. This is illegal and not encouraged.
B) Incorrect. Avoiding tax law is a punishable offense.
C) Incorrect. Family favors are illegal.
D) Correct. Keeping a list of incomes and expenses is the best way to have a good tax year.

64. A) Incorrect. Atherosclerosis is thickening of arterial walls.
B) Incorrect. Angina pectoralis is pain in the chest resulting from insufficient blood flow to the heart.
C) Correct. An embolism moves throughout the circulatory system, potentially lodging in the heart, lungs, or brain.
D) Incorrect. This describes a herniated disk is when spinal disk material protrudes beyond the vertebrae.

65. A) Incorrect. Spastic muscles can benefit from hot therapy.
B) Incorrect. Trigger points can benefit from hot therapy.
C) Correct. If the blood vessels are narrowed, hot therapy would only increase the volume of blood pressuring the walls, putting the client at risk.
D) Incorrect. Bound fascia can benefit from hot therapy.

66. **A) Correct.** The word root *opia* refers to vision. For example, myopia is a condition in which the patient has trouble seeing distant objects.
B) Incorrect. Breathing is described using the suffix –*pnea* as in apnea, the cessation of respiration, or the prefix *pneu*– as in pneumonia.
C) Incorrect. The word root that refers to the kidneys is *renal*. For instance, the adrenal glands are located above the kidneys: *ad*– (above) and *renal* (kidneys).
D) Incorrect. The word root for pain is *algia*, as in neuralgia.

67. A) Incorrect. The ileum contains clusters of lacteals to enhance fat absorption.
B) Correct. The jejunum is the second section of the small intestine.
C) Incorrect. The duodenum is where enzymes and bile produced by accessory organs are received.
D) Incorrect. The cecum is part of the colon.

68. A) Incorrect. Rate increases are determined using financial assessment tools.
B) Incorrect. A meeting with a supervisor does not imply the need for self-assessment.
C) Correct. A self-assessment technique is a good way to methodically think through a problematic situation and establish what to do if it occurs again.

	D)	Incorrect. Bringing on new staff involves a business assessment.

69.
- A) Incorrect. Cold therapy can promote homeostasis.
- B) Incorrect. Cold therapy can reduce pain.
- C) Incorrect. Cold therapy can reduce inflammation.
- **D) Correct.** Reynaud's disease and other circulatory issues contraindicate cold therapy.

70.
- **A) Correct.** *RICE* stands for Rest, Ice, Compression, Elevation.
- B) Incorrect. This is not the correct meaning of this acronym.
- C) Incorrect. Here, *RICE* has a different meaning.
- D) Incorrect. This is not the correct answer choice.

71.
- A) Incorrect. The therapist should stay professional and client centered.
- B) Incorrect. This would be rude, unprofessional, and insensitive.
- **C) Correct.** The therapist must obtain clearance and treatment recommendations from a physician.
- D) Incorrect. The therapist should know this is a contraindication for massage without medical clearance.

72.
- **A) Correct.** Proprioceptors can be found in the inner ear, synovial joints, skeletal framework, tendons, and muscle.
- B) Incorrect. Development of muscle memory and hand-eye coordination are related to proprioceptors.
- C) Incorrect. Muscle spindles sense muscle stretching and Golgi tendon organs sense muscle tension.
- D) Incorrect. Because of communication to the CNS, movements are coordinated.

73.
- **A) Correct.** A W-2 is for employees, not independent contractors.
- B) Incorrect. A W-9 is the form for independent contractors' taxes.
- C) Incorrect. Independent contractors should save a percentage of each check, since they will have to pay their own taxes.
- D) Incorrect. Independent contractors have to file and pay their own taxes each year.

74.
- A) Incorrect. A cross bridge is formed when myosin heads and actin attachment sites connect.
- B) Incorrect. A recovery stroke is when myosin heads move back into a resting position.
- **C) Correct.** Vasodilation occurs when the diameter of a blood vessel lumen enlarges.
- D) Incorrect. Communication between a muscle and the central nervous system results in an action potential.

75.
- **A) Correct.** Scheduling an appointment and showing up implies a client is consenting to receiving a massage.
- B) Incorrect. Voluntary consent is when a client has willingly, and not under duress, agreed to receive a massage based on a two-way conversation with the therapist.
- C) Incorrect. Informed consent is based on a client's voluntary agreement to massage after a therapist has reviewed the intake form with the client, gathered additional details, and recommended a treatment.
- D) Incorrect. There is no such term as *absolute consent* in massage therapy.

76.
- A) Incorrect. The therapist's elbow can be used as a tool during massage.
- B) Incorrect. The therapist's thumb can be used as a tool during massage.
- C) Incorrect. The therapist's forearm can be used as a tool during massage.
- **D) Correct.** The ninja star should not be used as a tool during massage, or anywhere outside of a ninja battle.

77.
- A) Incorrect. A hair strand is anatomically known as a hair shaft.

- B) Incorrect. What is usually called the fingernail is actually the nail plate.
- **C) Correct.** The eponychium provides a waterproof seal over the nail matrix and root.
- D) Incorrect. A hair follicle is a small tube-shaped crater in the epidermis.

78.
- A) Incorrect. Therapists should show off their good work ethic.
- **B) Correct.** A therapist should arrive wearing clean, unwrinkled clothing.
- C) Incorrect. Therapists should bring a copy of their resume to an interview.
- D) Incorrect. Therapists should bring their license, or a copy, to an interview.

79.
- A) Incorrect. Western medicine is rooted in science and evidence-based approaches.
- B) Incorrect. Allopathic medicine is synonymous with Western medicine practices.
- **C) Correct.** Many Eastern medicine practices are thousands of years old.
- D) Incorrect. Complementary and alternative medicine (CAM) is relatively new in Western medicine approaches to care. Treatment plans may incorporate nontraditional therapies and techniques.

80.
- A) Incorrect. Alveoli are located in the lungs.
- **B) Correct.** The epiglottis keeps food and liquid from entering the trachea.
- C) Incorrect. Hyaline cartilage keeps the trachea from collapsing and blocking air flow.
- D) Incorrect. The trachea bifurcates into the right and left bronchi.

81.
- A) Incorrect. This is not sports massage.
- **B) Correct.** Sports massage is designed with athletes and their performance in mind.
- C) Incorrect. This would be painful and ill-advised in any treatment.
- D) Incorrect. While lymph work may be a component of a certain sports massage, this definition is incorrect.

82.
- **A) Correct.** Employment reprimands should come directly from someone who is in a position of authority in the workplace.
- B) Incorrect. A workplace reprimand for a minor infraction may be in the form of a verbal warning.
- C) Incorrect. A workplace reprimand for a minor or major infraction may be in the form of a written warning.
- D) Incorrect. An employer may terminate employment on the spot if the infraction was a serious violation of workplace rules of conduct.

83.
- A) Incorrect. The heart meridian channel governs the mind and spirit.
- B) Incorrect. The gallbladder meridian channel ensures the smooth flow of chi and governs decision-making.
- **C) Correct.** The kidney channel is considered the root of life and stores essence.
- D) Incorrect. The liver channel is often considered the second heart.

84.
- A) Incorrect. Effleurage warms up tissue, making it more pliable during later stages of massage.
- B) Incorrect. Effleurage increases blood flow.
- **C) Correct.** Performed correctly, effleurage should lower stress levels.
- D) Incorrect. Effleurage encourages relaxation.

85.
- A) Incorrect. Babies do not receive relaxin's highest levels.
- B) Incorrect. The elderly do not receive relaxin's highest levels.
- **C) Correct.** Pregnant women receive relaxin's highest levels, especially during the first two weeks of pregnancy.
- D) Incorrect. Teenagers do not receive relaxin's highest levels.

86. A) Incorrect. The midsagittal (median) plane runs vertically down the midline of the body, dividing it equally into right and left sections.

B) Incorrect. The coronal (frontal) plane passes through the body, dividing it into anterior and posterior sections.

C) Correct. The transverse plane passes horizontally through the body, dividing it into superior and inferior sections.

D) Incorrect. The sagittal plane passes through the body parallel to the midsagittal plane.

87. A) Incorrect. It is a common rule in the workplace for employees to avoid using lewd or foul language.

B) Incorrect. An employer may legitimately expect employees to adhere to a standard dress code.

C) Correct. An employer cannot insist or require that employees work for free, regardless of the reason.

D) Incorrect. Speaking negatively about a coworker is unprofessional and bad for morale.

88. A) Incorrect. Using a company computer without permission from a supervisor would be a workplace violation, unless the computer is designated for massage therapists employed by the business.

B) Incorrect. Using a company-owned washer and dryer for personal laundry without permission would be a workplace violation.

C) Correct. An employer cannot insist employees work outside of their officially scheduled and agreed-upon hours.

D) Incorrect. Gathering personal client information for any reason would be a workplace violation.

89. A) Correct. Insurance helps protect massage therapists and their businesses from risk.

B) Incorrect. Not everyone is ill intentioned and looking to sue, but insurance is a good defense, just in case.

C) Incorrect. Massage therapists have to pay taxes regardless of whether they have insurance.

D) Incorrect. Having insurance does not allow massage therapists to sue their clients; furthermore, this is not a good business practice.

90. A) Incorrect. An angle is formed by two diverging lines.

B) Incorrect. A crest is a prominent elevation.

C) Incorrect. A meatus is an opening or canal.

D) Correct. A ramus is an arm or branch of a bone. The mandibular ramus is an example.

91. A) Incorrect. The cranial nerves are numbered using roman numerals one (I) through twelve (XII).

B) Incorrect. A human adult has seven cervical, twelve thoracic, and five lumbar vertebrae, for a total of twenty-four.

C) Correct. There are actually twelve pairs of ribs, not ten.

D) Incorrect. The human foot has seven tarsals, five metatarsals, and fourteen phalanges, for a total of twenty-six bones.

92. A) Incorrect. Crestor® is a drug that lowers cholesterol and slows the buildup of arterial plaque.

B) Correct. Vyvanse® treats attention deficit hyperactivity disorder (ADHD) in adults and children, as well as binge eating disorder. It can be habit forming.

C) Incorrect. Lyrica® treats diabetic nerve pain, fibromyalgia, spinal cord nerve pain resulting from injury, and persistent nerve pain resulting from having shingles. It is also used as an accompaniment to epileptic drugs.

D) Incorrect. Coumadin® is an anticoagulant, or blood thinner.

93. A) Incorrect. A protuberance is a bulge.

B) Incorrect. A facet guides and limits motion.

- C) **Correct.** A foramen is a hole in a bone for nerves or vessels to pass through. The obturator foramen of the pelvis is one example.
- D) Incorrect. A spine is a narrow, slender projection.

94.
- A) Incorrect. Lymphatic drainage massage can reduce swelling and edema.
- B) Incorrect. Lymphatic drainage massage can assist a client in recovery from surgery.
- C) **Correct.** Lymphatic drainage massage is a light treatment and does not release trigger points.
- D) Incorrect. Lymphatic drainage massage can increase energy.

95.
- A) Incorrect. This type of conversation is not acceptable at all in the workplace.
- B) Incorrect. Management will not consider this appropriate and will want to take further action than disallowing the therapist to perform massages on this client again.
- C) **Correct.** The employer will prepare a written explanation of why the behavior was inappropriate and have the therapist sign it.
- D) Incorrect. If the therapist's coworker did this, she would be in violation as well.

96.
- A) Incorrect. Business plans are used to set realistic goals.
- B) Incorrect. Business plans should not be used to beg for money; they present investors with an opportunity.
- C) **Correct.** A business plan is a model covering all aspects of operations and can be used to obtain loans.
- D) Incorrect. A business plan is more for the business's owners and principal lenders.

97.
- A) Incorrect. Lateral rotator muscles laterally rotate the hip.
- B) Incorrect. Quadriceps femoris muscles primarily extend the knee.
- C) Incorrect. There are three hamstring muscles.

- D) **Correct.** The pectineus originates from the superior ramus of pubis and inserts at the pectineal line of femur. The muscles of the adductor group primarily adduct and medially rotate the hip. The other four muscles in the adductor group are the gracilis and the adductor brevis, longus, and magnus.

98.
- A) Incorrect. Earth contains metal.
- B) **Correct.** Water nourishes wood.
- C) Incorrect. Metal collects water.
- D) Incorrect. Fire produces earth.

99.
- A) **Correct.** Proprioception helps with spatial sensation and navigation.
- B) Incorrect. Proprioception may help with the ability to move, but it is not the primary definition.
- C) Incorrect. Perception is the ability to gain awareness through any of the senses.
- D) Incorrect. Nociception is the ability to sense pain.

100.
- A) Incorrect. Irregular bones do not fit into any classification.
- B) Incorrect. Sesamoid bones are small and roundish.
- C) **Correct.** Short bones provide support and stability with little movement.
- D) Incorrect. Long bones have a length that greatly exceeds their width.

THREE: Practice Test Three

Read the question carefully and choose the most correct answer.

1. In ancient tribal societies, *shaman* was another name for what?
   A) demon
   B) doctor
   C) healer
   D) disease

2. What is the name of the cells that transport oxygen through the circulatory system?
   A) leukocytes
   B) thrombocytes
   C) arterioles
   D) erythrocytes

3. Why is HIPAA used by massage professionals?
   A) Massage therapists are doctors.
   B) Massage therapists deal with clients' private information.
   C) Massage therapists like to talk about clients to their friends.
   D) Massage therapists do not know how to follow rules.

4. The tunica intima, tunica media, and tunica externa are layers of what structure(s)?
   A) heart
   B) arteries and veins
   C) capillaries
   D) purkinje fibers

5. Why is self-assessment a valuable technique in massage?
   A) It allows a client to feel empowered when it comes to treatment.
   B) It allows a therapist to informally diagnose a client's condition.
   C) It gives the therapist the opportunity to recognize areas where boundaries are at risk.
   D) It indicates to a client when to schedule a massage.

6. Which of the following methods were NOT used by shamans for healing?
   A) herbs
   B) surgery
   C) touch
   D) steam

7. Synthroid® is used to treat what condition?
   A) anxiety and panic disorders
   B) hypothyroidism
   C) seizures and nerve pain
   D) gastroesophageal reflux disease

8. What is homeostasis?
   A) the ability of the body to find its way home when lost
   B) the ability of the body to regulate balance
   C) the ability of the body to deregulate balance
   D) the ability of the body to know when not to move

9. The practice of amma began where?
   A) China
   B) Japan
   C) India
   D) Greece

10. Who was the Greek god of medicine and healing?
    A) Asclepius
    B) Herodicus
    C) Celsus
    D) Hippocrates

11. What is the name of the fibrous sac that surrounds and protects the heart?
    A) aorta
    B) pericardium
    C) pulmonary trunk
    D) venous pump

12. Where does the alimentary canal begin and end?
    A) It begins at the oral cavity and ends in the large intestine.
    B) It begins in the pharynx and ends at the anus.
    C) It begins at the oral cavity and ends at the anus.
    D) It begins in the stomach and ends at the anus.

13. Which of the following is NOT a benefit of receiving massage?
    A) better quality of sleep
    B) increased stress levels
    C) increased range of motion
    D) decreased tension headaches

14. What does HIPAA's Privacy Rule protect?
    A) a massage therapist's privacy
    B) the security of a massage therapist's health information
    C) a client's right not to share her information
    D) a client's privacy and the security of her health information

15. Anatripsis refers to what technique?
    A) equine massage
    B) rubbing
    C) a technique used to balance bodily fluids
    D) energy balancing used by shamans

16. A therapist has a right to refuse to massage a client for all of the following reasons EXCEPT:
    A) improper hygiene
    B) personal safety
    C) contraindications
    D) sexual orientation

17. Which of the following is an autoimmune disorder that attacks connective tissue in the body?

- A) multiple sclerosis (MS)
- B) lupus
- C) rheumatoid arthritis
- D) Crohn's disease

18. What part(s) of the alimentary canal makes up the middle gastrointestinal tract?

- A) small intestine
- B) the stomach
- C) the esophagus and the stomach
- D) small intestine and the colon

19. What is the digestive purpose of the liver?

- A) absorption
- B) peristalsis
- C) form a bolus
- D) produce bile

20. Sweat, salivary, mammary, sebaceous, and mucous are what type of glands?

- A) hormonal
- B) exocrine
- C) negative feedback
- D) endocrine

21. How should massage therapists handle clients' private information?

- A) make copies and share the records with their neighbors
- B) burn or shred records after a client leaves the office
- C) store in a secure location, in a client's properly marked file for a period of ten years
- D) store in a haphazard, unmarked file cabinet

22. Which of the following is NOT a mechanism that controls hormone levels?

- A) hormonal control
- B) Islets of Langerhans
- C) neural control
- D) negative feedback

23. What precautions should a therapist take when working with a client with an open sore or dermatitis?

- A) A therapist should use vinyl or latex gloves when working with a client with an open sore or dermatitis.
- B) A therapist should put a Band-Aid on a client's open sore.
- C) A therapist should refuse to work on a client with dermatitis.
- D) A therapists should call in sick if he has a cut on his finger.

24. What is a trigger point?

- A) the ball of the foot
- B) a hypoirritable spot in a muscle
- C) a bone in the thumb
- D) a hyperirritable spot in a taut band of muscle

25. If a massage therapist is late for work and another therapist had to perform her massage, what should she say to management?

- A) "Oh well, at least someone else was available to do the massage."
- B) "The therapist that did the massage is new and needs the money."
- C) "I overslept; it happens. The massage got done, didn't it?"
- D) "I am really sorry for the inconvenience. I hope the client was happy with the massage he received."

26. Which of the following should NOT be included on a client's intake form?
    A) reason for visit
    B) client's contact information
    C) client's social media information
    D) insurance information

27. The pineal gland produces what hormone?
    A) melatonin
    B) cortisol
    C) calcitonin
    D) human growth hormone

28. What is the purpose of melanin in the epidermis?
    A) waterproof and protect
    B) produce sebum
    C) produce collagen
    D) provide UV protection and determine skin pigment

29. What are the benefits of cryotherapy?
    A) vasodilation
    B) vasoconstriction
    C) increased inflammation
    D) increased lymph flow

30. What is one way of practicing self-care?
    A) going to the bar
    B) scheduling a busy day with no breaks
    C) stretching and exercising regularly
    D) crying into a pillow

31. Which is the INCORRECT statement related to hair follicles?
    A) They are contained in the epidermis.
    B) Hair follicles are formed continuously during a lifetime.
    C) The human body has hair follicles that number in the millions.
    D) Hair follicles are held in place by arrector pili.

32. Which governmental body has influence on the practice of massage?
    A) state
    B) none
    C) federal
    D) city

33. Who learned about muscular contraction through dissection?
    A) William Harvey
    B) Ambroise Paré
    C) Timothy Bright
    D) Giovanni Alfonso Borelli

34. Which of the following is a physical response to the sympathetic nervous system?
    A) contract the bladder
    B) stimulate saliva production
    C) increase heart rate
    D) increase stomach digestion

35. What occurs in the proliferative phase of wound healing?
    A) Vasodilation of blood vessels occurs.
    B) A temporary protective barrier is formed.
    C) A scar forms.
    D) The healing process is completed.

36. What is NOT a function of the lymphatic system?

- **A)** It drains excess interstitial fluid.
- **B)** It transports fats and fat-soluble vitamins.
- **C)** It transports and distributes gases.
- **D)** It aids the immune system.

37. What is the importance of an intake form?

- **A)** to collect a client's information and define what is expected in the massage treatment
- **B)** to collect a client's information to become friends
- **C)** to collect a client's information to share with other professionals
- **D)** to collect a client's information to use his identity

38. Which of the following is a safety hazard in a therapy room?

- **A)** sheets folded and properly stored in a cabinet
- **B)** rugs or cords that are taped down on the floor
- **C)** a table warmer cord that runs next to the table
- **D** a chair that sits in the corner

39. What type of massage is considered the foundation of many other types of massage?

- **A)** Swedish massage
- **B)** sports massage
- **C)** deep tissue massage
- **D)** prenatal massage

40. Which of the following is a degenerative disorder that causes the brain to shrink and neural tissue to die?

- **A)** Parkinson's disease
- **B)** transient ischemic attack (TIA)
- **C)** Raynaud's syndrome
- **D)** Alzheimer's disease

41. What are the bean-shaped structures in the lymphatic system?

- **A)** lymph nodes
- **B)** Peyer's patches
- **C)** tonsils
- **D)** lymphatic trunks

42. Which is the largest of all the secondary lymphatic structures?

- **A)** vermiform appendix
- **B)** cisterna chyli
- **C)** thymus
- **D)** spleen

43. What deep, sustained technique's goal is to spread muscle fibers, soften tight muscles, and increase lymphatic flow and circulation in the area being treated?

- **A)** effleurage
- **B)** petrissage
- **C)** stroking
- **D)** compression

44. What does endomysium cover?

- **A)** an individual muscle fiber
- **B)** bundles of muscle fibers
- **C)** an entire muscle
- **D)** fascicles

45. Which of the following is NOT a type of muscle manipulation technique?
    A) percussion
    B) effleurage
    C) petrissage
    D) punching

46. Which of the following do therapists working within a scope of practice NOT need to do?
    A) protect the public
    B) be accountable
    C) assess their competency
    D) be licensed by the state in which they are practicing

47. At what point in the SOAP notes should the acronym OL' DR. FICARA be used for gathering information from the client?
    A) Subjective
    B) Objective
    C) Assessment
    D) Plan

48. What does the mnemonic device *Clean The Baby's Nose* stand for?
    A) Cold, Tingling, Burning, Numbness
    B) Cool, Twinging, Blistering, Numbness
    C) Cold, Twitching, Burning, Numbness
    D) Cold, Tingling, Burning, Nerve damage

49. Which of the following is NOT related to the spine?
    A) kyphosis
    B) lordosis
    C) gout
    D) scoliosis

50. What type of muscle contracts in order to move and push the contents of an organ?
    A) cardiac
    B) neuromuscular
    C) skeletal
    D) smooth

51. What wraps around a sarcolemma like a ring on a finger?
    A) I band
    B) t-tubules
    C) zone of overlap
    D) myosin

52. Can a massage therapist prescribe to or diagnose a client?
    A) no
    B) yes
    C) sometimes
    D) only when the doctor is out of the office

53. Which of the following is the best example of implied consent?
    A) entering the massage room with the therapist
    B) filling out and signing the intake form
    C) agreeing to a treatment plan recommended by the therapist
    D) disrobing

54. What is the blood-brain barrier?
    A) one of the layers of the meninges
    B) surrounds the cerebrospinal fluid
    C) keeps blood and cerebrospinal fluid separated
    D) another name for the central nervous system

55. Neurotransmitters are spilled into what aspect of the synapse?

   A) postsynaptic
   B) presynaptic
   C) nodes of Ranvier
   D) synaptic cleft

56. What is NOT a region of the brain?

   A) cerebrum
   B) cerebellum
   C) neuroglia
   D) diencephalon

57. What do seminal vesicles contribute?

   A) 20 to 30 percent of semen
   B) 10 percent of semen
   C) They are the sole source of sperm.
   D) 60 percent of semen

58. What is the difference between friction and cross-fiber friction work?

   A) There is no difference.
   B) Friction uses a heat tool and cross-fiber uses a therapist's hands.
   C) Friction is performed with the direction of muscle fibers and cross-fiber friction uses superficial tissues to scrub against deeper tissues.
   D) Friction uses superficial tissue to scrub against deeper tissues and cross-fiber friction is performed with the direction of muscle fibers.

59. What feel-good hormone can touch release in the recipient?

   A) cortisol
   B) relaxin
   C) oxytocin
   D) dopamine

60. What is the term for veins whose valves are not functioning properly and therefore not returning blood to the heart?

   A) valvular veins
   B) varicose veins
   C) lymphatic beds
   D) spider veins

61. What is NOT a benefit of the massage therapist starting a massage at the head and neck?

   A) The therapist has a moment to get centered and focused on the client's massage session.
   B) The therapist can work for several minutes before undraping needs to occur.
   C) The client can get adjusted to the therapist's touch before undraping occurs.
   D) The therapist can do a final check to see if he has any new text messages.

62. In which of the following cases are SOAP notes NOT shared?

   A) in court when discussing a case involving treatment
   B) when talking to a client's doctor about a comprehensive treatment plan
   C) at a dinner party
   D) when talking to a fellow massage therapist who also sees the client

63. Which of the following is also called a popliteal cyst?

   A) Baker's cyst
   B) ganglion cyst
   C) lipoma
   D) wart

PRACTICE TEST THREE

64. Which of the following massage modalities does NOT use compression?

- **A)** acupressure
- **B)** shiatsu
- **C)** healing touch
- **D)** trigger point

65. What is one of the primary roles of estrogen in reproduction?

- **A)** assist with the maturation of oocytes
- **B)** richly supply the endometrium with blood
- **C)** create a barrier in the vagina to deter sperm
- **D)** trigger ovulation

66. In massage, which of the following techniques is a Swedish gymnastic technique?

- **A)** kneading
- **B)** gliding
- **C)** vibration
- **D)** joint mobilization

67. What is commonly referred to as the voice box?

- **A)** trachea
- **B)** pharynx
- **C)** larynx
- **D)** frontal sinus

68. Workplace rules will generally cover all of the following but one. Which one?

- **A)** day-to-day responsibilities
- **B)** procedures
- **C)** professional conduct
- **D)** permitted instances of sexual relations between coworkers outside of business hours

69. What is one difference between hydraulic and stationary tables?

- **A)** Hydraulic tables are submerged in water.
- **B)** Stationary tables can never be moved.
- **C)** Hydraulic tables can be adjusted while the client is on the table.
- **D)** Stationary tables can be adjusted while the client is on the table.

70. What are c-shaped rings?

- **A)** the epiglottis
- **B)** alveolar sacs
- **C)** cilia
- **D)** hyaline cartilage

71. Which describes the respiratory diaphragm?

- **A)** During expiration, the diaphragm contracts.
- **B)** During inspiration, the diaphragm relaxes.
- **C)** The diaphragm separates the thoracic cavity from the abdominal cavity.
- **D)** The respiratory diaphragm contains millions of alveoli.

72. Which of the following modalities is water based?

- **A)** zero balancing
- **B)** hot stone therapy
- **C)** Watsu
- **D)** Esalen

73. Which of the following is considered a light-touch modality?

- **A)** ashiatsu
- **B)** Rolfing
- **C)** sports massage
- **D)** craniosacral

74. States will generally allow all of the following topical applications used during massage except one. Which one?

- **A)** salt and sugar
- **B)** hot wax for hair removal
- **C)** water
- **D)** herbal products

75. Which statement about types of connective tissue is NOT correct?

- **A)** Osseous tissue is bone that is considered dead.
- **B)** Cartilage is firm but flexible.
- **C)** Ligaments are fibrous and elastic.
- **D)** Bone marrow is soft and spongy and found in the medullary cavity of long bones.

76. When a coworker comes to a therapist for a massage and discloses that she takes medication for a mental illness, what should the therapist do?

- **A)** Treat this information the same way the therapist would with any other client.
- **B)** Let the coworker know she is not alone and the therapist is always available if she wants to talk.
- **C)** After the massage, immediately contact the therapist's supervisor and disclose this information for safety and security purposes.
- **D)** Tell the coworker about a family member who took the same medication and had really bad side effects.

77. What is the benefit of a massage therapist knowing bony landmarks?

- **A)** They are endangerment sites and should be avoided.
- **B)** They can be very painful to a client if pressure is put on them.
- **C)** They can be easily palpated.
- **D)** They can indicate if a client is developing osteoporosis.

78. What is hematopoiesis?

- **A)** a blood disease
- **B)** part of a long bone
- **C)** the process of producing blood cells
- **D)** a condition that occurs when bone becomes more porous

79. Which of the following is NOT a determining factor for adjusting table height?

- **A)** the height of the therapist
- **B)** the weight of the client
- **C)** the height of the client
- **D)** the type of massage treatment

80. Which of the following is considered an internal foreign invader?

- **A)** viruses
- **B)** fungi
- **C)** cellular debris
- **D)** parasites

81. How are autoimmune diseases defined?

- **A)** as a genetic influence
- **B)** an allergic reaction
- **C)** a result of the hygiene hypothesis
- **D)** when immune cells attack themselves

82. When does urination occur?
    A) when the urethra receives the urine
    B) when urine reaches the bladder
    C) when ureters receive the urine
    D) after the kidneys filter out waste

83. When using contrast therapy, what is the ratio for heat-to-cold duration?
    A) 2:1
    B) 3:3
    C) 1:3
    D) 3:1

84. Who was Pehr Henrik Ling?
    A) creator of the Swedish movement cure
    B) a Dutch physician
    C) a doctor who opened an orthopedic practice in the United States
    D) the author of *A Practical Treatise on Massage*

85. A therapist is grocery shopping one day and runs into a client. What type of dual relationship is this?
    A) communal
    B) social
    C) family and close friends
    D) work-based

86. Which of the following is NOT part of the OSHA mission?
    A) saving lives
    B) preventing injuries
    C) protesting inequality
    D) protecting the health of American workers

87. Which one of the following is NOT associated with the respiratory system?
    A) *–plegia*
    B) emphysema
    C) cystic fibrosis
    D) asthma

88. Which of the following is the result of long term dysfunction of, and damage to, liver cells?
    A) cirrhosis
    B) celiac disease
    C) cellulitis
    D) Grave's disease

89. Which of the following is NOT a benefit of hot therapy?
    A) vasodilation
    B) vasoconstriction
    C) increased blood flow and lymph flow
    D) decreased nerve firings

90. How is the urge to urinate communicated?
    A) when waste is classified as urine
    B) when the ureters transport urine in the urinary bladder
    C) by receptors in the bladder walls
    D) when blood pH is out of balance

91. When should therapists leave the room when using hot therapy?
    A) after ten minutes
    B) only if they really have to go to the bathroom
    C) never
    D) after the first application

92. Which may be the repercussion of an employee talking about a "hot" client in the break room of a place of business?

- **A)** None. It is okay as long as the conversation is with a coworker the therapist is friends with outside of work.
- **B)** Management informs the therapist he or she will no longer be allowed to massage that client.
- **C)** The therapist may receive a written warning of termination by his employer.
- **D)** The coworker will schedule a massage with that client and tell the client the therapist is awesome.

93. The three treasures are related to which Eastern medicine practice?

- **A)** Ayurveda
- **B)** yin/yang
- **C)** shiatsu
- **D)** traditional Chinese medicine

94. Why is it important to wash sheets at 160 degrees Fahrenheit?

- **A)** Sheets can actually be washed in hot or cold water.
- **B)** Hot water kills pathogens.
- **C)** Sheets should actually be washed in colder water because it is better for the environment.
- **D)** Cold water cleans stains better.

95. Which of the following is commonly referred to as *frozen shoulder*?

- **A)** bursitis
- **B)** dislocation
- **C)** trigeminal neuralgia
- **D)** adhesive capsulitis

96. Which term is NOT associated with Ayurveda?

- **A)** eight pillars
- **B)** life knowledge
- **C)** dosha
- **D)** acupressure points

97. Crown, sacral, and third eye are related to what Eastern medicine practice?

- **A)** healing touch
- **B)** chakra balancing
- **C)** polarity therapy
- **D)** acupressure

98. Who wrote the book *The Art of Massage*?

- **A)** Hartvig Nissen
- **B)** Charles Fayette Taylor
- **C)** John Harvey Kellogg
- **D)** Pehr Henrik Ling

99. When should a treatment room be disinfected?

- **A)** at the therapist's discretion
- **B)** before and after each treatment
- **C)** when the boss schedules a cleaning crew
- **D)** weekly

100. Which of the following is the medical term for *ringworm*?

- **A)** impetigo
- **B)** phlebitis
- **C)** tinea
- **D)** varicose vein

PRACTICE TEST THREE ANSWER KEY

1.
   A) Incorrect. A demon was something that was associated with illness and disease.
   B) Incorrect. The word *doctor* was not associated with shamanism.
   C) **Correct.** A shaman was viewed as a healer.
   D) Incorrect. A disease was something a shaman attempted to heal through ritual.

2.
   A) Incorrect. Leukocytes are white blood cells that protect the body from bacteria, viruses, and other pathogens.
   B) Incorrect. Thrombocytes are cells sent to repair damaged vessels by clotting the blood.
   C) Incorrect. Arterioles are vessels that branch off from arteries.
   D) **Correct.** Erythrocytes are red blood cells that transport oxygen.

3.
   A) Incorrect. Massage therapists are not doctors; they have a different scope of practice.
   B) **Correct.** Massage therapists deal with clients' private information and, as such, use HIPAA's guidelines to protect their clients.
   C) Incorrect. Massage therapists should not discuss their clients with their friends.
   D) Incorrect. Massage therapists use HIPAA as a guideline for proper management of clients' private information.

4.
   A) Incorrect. The endocardium, myocardium, and epicardium are the layers of the heart walls.
   B) **Correct.** The tunica intima is the innermost layer, the tunica media is the middle layer, and the tunica externa is the outermost layer of arteries and veins.
   C) Incorrect. Capillaries are thin, membranous vessels that move blood slowly.
   D) Incorrect. Purkinje fibers cause impulses to spread through the myocardium.

5.
   A) Incorrect. Voluntary and informed consent empower a client.
   B) Incorrect. A therapist may not formally or informally diagnose a client's condition.
   C) **Correct.** Self-assessment allows therapists to focus on their role as massage therapists.
   D) Incorrect. There is no formal tool used to help a client determine when to schedule a massage.

6.
   A) Incorrect. Herbs were used in shamanic healing.
   B) **Correct.** Surgery, as we know it today, was not used by shamans.
   C) Incorrect. Touch was used in shamanic healing.
   D) Incorrect. Generating steam was used in shamanic healing.

7.
   A) Incorrect. Niravam® and Xanax®, also referred to as alprazolam, are used to treat anxiety and panic disorders.
   B) **Correct.** Synthroid® is an oral, synthetic hormone replacement drug used to treat hypothyroidism. It is also referred to as levothyroxine.
   C) Incorrect. Neurontin®, also referred to as gabapentin, is an antiepileptic medication used to treat seizures as well as shingles-based nerve pain.
   D) Incorrect. Nexium®, also referred to as esomeprazole, is used to treat GERD and other gastrointestinal disorders.

8.
   A) Incorrect. Homeostasis does not navigate.
   B) **Correct.** Homeostasis regulates balance in the body.
   C) Incorrect. Homeostasis regulates toward balance.
   D) Incorrect. Homeostasis does not control movement.

9.
   A) **Correct.** Amma is a system of manual and energy techniques that originated in China.

B) Incorrect. Amma spread to Japan from China.

C) Incorrect. Ayurveda is a health and treatment system developed in India.

D) Incorrect. Amma is not associated with Greece.

10. **A) Correct.** Asclepius is best known today by his symbol, the rod of Asclepius, a snake-entwined staff.

B) Incorrect. Herodicus was a Greek doctor.

C) Incorrect. Celsus was a Roman physician who wrote *De Medicina*.

D) Incorrect. Hippocrates is considered the father of medicine.

11. A) Incorrect. The aorta is the primary artery that receives blood from the heart.

B) Correct. The pericardium is also called the pericardial sac.

C) Incorrect. The pulmonary trunk extends upward from the heart and is part of the pulmonary circuit.

D) Incorrect. The venous pump is a valve system in veins.

12. A) Incorrect. It does begin at the oral cavity; the large intestine is a part of the alimentary canal but not the end.

B) Incorrect. The pharynx is a part of the alimentary canal but not the beginning; it does end at the anus.

C) Correct. The oral cavity is where ingestion begins and the anus is where excretion occurs.

D) Incorrect. The stomach is a part of the alimentary canal but not the beginning; it does end at the anus.

13. A) Incorrect. Massage does promote better sleep quality.

B) Correct. Massage decreases stress levels.

C) Incorrect. The effects of massage do increase range of motion on treated muscles and joints.

D) Incorrect. Massage has been linked to decreased tension headaches in headache sufferers.

14. A) Incorrect. The Privacy Rule does not protect massage therapists.

B) Incorrect. The Privacy Rule does not cover a massage therapist as the provider.

C) Incorrect. The Privacy Rule does not protect a client's unwillingness to share information.

D) Correct. The Privacy Rule protects a client's right to privacy and the security of her health information.

15. A) Incorrect. Avicenna believed in using friction techniques for grooming horses.

B) Correct. Hippocrates used the word *anatripsis* to describe rubbing.

C) Incorrect. Hippocrates believed that bodily fluids needed to be balanced; anatripsis was one technique used to accomplish this balance.

D) Incorrect. *Anatripsis* was a term that was not known to shamans.

16. A) Incorrect. Extremely poor personal hygiene can be an indicator of both mental and physical illness.

B) Incorrect. Therapists do not have to proceed if they have justifiable concerns that their health and wellness may be at risk.

C) Incorrect. Proceeding with a massage when it is contraindicated by information obtained from the client violates the healthcare practitioner's do no harm ethic.

D) Correct. Not massaging someone solely based on sexual orientation is discriminatory.

17. A) Incorrect. MS targets the central nervous system.

B) Correct. Lupus can affect any connective tissue in the body.

C) Incorrect. Rheumatoid arthritis occurs when the synovial fluid in a joint is attacked by the immune system.

	D)	Incorrect. Crohn's disease affects the gastrointestinal tract.
18.	A)	**Correct.** The small intestine is the only part of the middle gastrointestinal tract.
	B)	Incorrect. The stomach is part of the upper gastrointestinal tract.
	C)	Incorrect. The esophagus and the stomach are both part of the upper gastrointestinal tract.
	D)	Incorrect. The small intestine is correct but the colon is the lower gastrointestinal tract.
19.	A)	Incorrect. Absorption is one of the functions of the digestive system.
	B)	Incorrect. Peristalsis is a series of muscular contractions that move digested food.
	C)	Incorrect. A bolus is a masticated lump formed using saliva.
	D)	**Correct.** Bile is an emulsifier produced by the liver to break apart large fat globules.
20.	A)	Incorrect. There are no hormonal glands.
	B)	**Correct.** Exocrine glands have ducts and do not feed directly into the bloodstream.
	C)	Incorrect. Negative feedback is a mechanism that controls hormonal levels.
	D)	Incorrect. Endocrine glands are ductless and secrete hormones directly into the bloodstream.
21.	A)	Incorrect. Clients' records should not be shared with non-medical professionals.
	B)	Incorrect. Clients' records should be stored for ten years.
	C)	**Correct.** Clients' records should be properly marked and stored for ten years.
	D)	Incorrect. Clients' records should be stored in a properly marked file in a secure location.
22.	A)	Incorrect. Hormonal control is one of three mechanisms that control hormone levels.
	B)	**Correct.** Islets of Langerhans are small groups of endocrine cells found in the pancreas.
	C)	Incorrect. Neural control is one of three mechanisms that control hormone levels.
	D)	Incorrect. Negative feedback is one of three mechanisms that control hormone levels.
23.	**A)**	**Correct.** Therapists should use gloves if they, or their client, have an open sore or dermatitis.
	B)	Incorrect. A therapist should not put a Band-Aid on a client's open sore.
	C)	Incorrect. A therapist can work on a client with dermatitis but should check with the client to make sure she is comfortable and adjust the treatment to the client's responses.
	D)	Incorrect. A therapist can still work if he has a cut on his finger, but he should wear gloves.
24.	A)	Incorrect. A trigger point is not a specific area.
	B)	Incorrect. The correct term is *hyperirritable*; the prefix *hypo–* is not used.
	C)	Incorrect. A trigger point is not a bone.
	D)	**Correct.** This is the correct definition of a trigger point.
25.	A)	Incorrect. This response shows a total lack of respect for the employer.
	B)	Incorrect. This response is an insult to the employer and the coworker who did the massage.
	C)	Incorrect. This response displays an absolute lack of professionalism and communication skills.
	D)	**Correct.** This response relays regret, acknowledges the impact of the action on others, and shows concern for the client. However, if tardiness becomes repetitive behavior, this regret will be

insincere and will most likely impact the therapist's position in the company.

26. A) Incorrect. An intake form should include the reason for a client's visit.
    B) Incorrect. An intake form should have the client's contact information.
    C) Correct. An intake form does not include a client's private social media information.
    D) Incorrect. An intake form should include insurance information, if insurance is accepted.

27. **A) Correct.** Melatonin helps to regulate the circadian rhythm.
    B) Incorrect. Cortisol is produced by the cortex layer of the adrenal glands.
    C) Incorrect. Calcitonin is produced by the thyroid gland.
    D) Incorrect. Human growth hormone is produce by the anterior pituitary gland.

28. A) Incorrect. Waterproofing and protection are the purposes of keratin.
    B) Incorrect. Sebum is produced by the sebaceous glands.
    C) Incorrect. Collagen is a group of structural proteins found throughout the body and makes up most of the dermis layer.
    D) Correct. Melanin is produced by melanocytes.

29. A) Incorrect. Vasodilation occurs with heat application.
    B) Correct. Vasoconstriction occurs with cold therapy.
    C) Incorrect. Cold therapy decreases inflammation.
    D) Incorrect. Cold therapy decreases lymph flow to the area.

30. A) Incorrect. Drinking is not a healthy way of practicing self-care.
    B) Incorrect. Overscheduling does not promote self-care.
    C) Correct. Regular stretching and exercise promote a healthy body and mind.
    D) Incorrect. While this may feel cathartic, there are better ways to practice self-care more consistently, such as breathing exercises or yoga.

31. A) Incorrect. Hair follicles are contained in the epidermis but are nourished by the dermis layer.
    B) Correct. Hair follicles are developed in the womb. After birth, no new follicles are developed.
    C) Incorrect. The human body does have millions of hair follicles.
    D) Incorrect. Arrector pili are small muscles. Each hair follicle is held in place by one of these muscles.

32. **A) Correct.** Each state determines the legal and professional rules that govern the practice of massage.
    B) Incorrect. While some states do not regulate the practice of massage, most of them do.
    C) Incorrect. The federal government has minimal oversight of the practice of massage.
    D) Incorrect. Most cities adhere to state laws, but some may have additional guidelines and requirements.

33. A) Incorrect. William Harvey discovered how blood circulates.
    B) Incorrect. Ambroise Paré, a military surgeon, found the orthopedic benefits of massage.
    C) Incorrect. Timothy Bright wrote about the value of baths, exercise, and massage.
    D) Correct. Giovanni Alfonso Borelli was an Italian physician.

34. A) Incorrect. The sympathetic nervous system relaxes the bladder.
    B) Incorrect. The sympathetic nervous system decreases saliva production.
    C) Correct. The sympathetic nervous system increases heart rate.
    D) Incorrect. The sympathetic nervous system decreases stomach digestion.

35.
- A) Incorrect. Vasodilation occurs in the inflammatory phase so healing aids can be rushed to the wound site.
- B) Incorrect. A temporary protective barrier is formed during the epithelialization phase.
- C) **Correct.** In the proliferative phase, the wound begins to fill in with new tissue that forms a lining in the bed of the wound, allowing a scar to form.
- D) Incorrect. The healing process is completed in the remodeling phase.

36.
- A) Incorrect. Excess interstitial fluid from body tissues is drained by the lymphatic system.
- B) Incorrect. Fat and fat-soluble vitamins from the digestive tract are transported by the lymphatic system.
- C) **Correct.** Transporting and distributing gases is a function of the circulatory and respiratory systems.
- D) Incorrect. The immune system relies heavily on the lymphatic system.

37.
- A) **Correct.** An intake form should provide the massage therapist with information to start a professional relationship with the client and should outline the treatment plan.
- B) Incorrect. A therapist should not use a client's information to start a friendship with the client.
- C) Incorrect. A therapist should treat the client's information as confidential and only share it in accordance with HIPAA; furthermore, the primary purpose of an intake form is to gather information for the massage therapist.
- D) Incorrect. It is unlawful to steal someone's identity, and therapists should not abuse their power.

38.
- A) Incorrect. Sheets that are folded and put in a cabinet do not pose a hazard to the therapist or client.
- B) Incorrect. Rugs or cords that are taped down on the floor reduce the risk of tripping and do not pose a hazard to the therapist or client.
- C) **Correct.** A cord that is not taped down can pose a hazard to the therapist or client.
- D) Incorrect. A chair that is not in the walking path of the therapist or client does not pose a hazard.

39.
- A) **Correct.** Swedish massage is a common practice in the West; many other types of massage are rooted in this modality.
- B) Incorrect. Sports massage uses Swedish techniques such as rocking or compressions.
- C) Incorrect. Deep tissue massage incorporates Swedish techniques in its treatment approach.
- D) Incorrect. Prenatal massage is similar to Swedish massage, but the therapist needs special training and certification in order to perform it on a client.

40.
- A) Incorrect. Parkinson's disease is a neurological degenerative brain disorder in which production of the neurotransmitter dopamine decreases over time.
- B) Incorrect. A TIA occurs when a small blood clot briefly blocks the flow of blood to the brain before breaking up or dissolving.
- C) Incorrect. Raynaud's syndrome occurs when arterial vessels spasm causing vasodilation and inhibiting the flow of blood to fingers and toes.
- D) **Correct.** Alzheimer's disease is mostly found in the elderly and presents as memory loss, deterioration of language and cognitive skills, disorientation, and ultimately in the inability care for oneself.

41.
- A) **Correct.** Lymph nodes are located all along the lymphatic vessels.
- B) Incorrect. Peyer's patches are nodules found in the small intestine.
- C) Incorrect. Tonsils are a group of lymph nodules.
- D) Incorrect. Lymphatic trunks feed cleansed lymph into one of two ducts.

42.
- A) Incorrect. The vermiform appendix is located in the lower-right quadrant of the abdomen.
- B) Incorrect. The cisterna chyli is a dilated sac that collects lymph.
- C) Incorrect. The thymus is a primary lymphatic structure.
- **D) Correct.** The spleen plays multiple supporting roles in the body.

43.
- A) Incorrect. Effleurage's long, fluid strokes are used to warm up superficial tissues.
- B) Incorrect. Petrissage focuses on deeper strokes based on effleurage-style techniques.
- C) Incorrect. Stroking is used to help the client get used to the therapist's touch, and for the therapist to move fluidly from area to area.
- **D) Correct.** Compressions are long, sustained pressure techniques designed to slowly warm up and spread muscle fibers.

44.
- **A) Correct.** An individual muscle fiber is surrounded by endomysium.
- B) Incorrect. Bundles of muscle fibers are surrounded by perimysium.
- C) Incorrect. A muscle is surrounded by epimysium.
- D) Incorrect. Fascicles are bundles of muscle fibers.

45.
- A) Incorrect. Percussion is a type of muscle manipulation technique.
- B) Incorrect. Effleurage is a type of muscle manipulation technique.
- C) Incorrect. Petrissage is a type of muscle manipulation technique.
- **D) Correct.** Punching is not a type of muscle manipulation technique.

46.
- A) Incorrect. A scope of practice limits practitioners to provide only those services in which they are adequately trained.
- B) Incorrect. A scope of practice includes an expectation of accountability by the practitioner.
- C) Incorrect. A scope of practice requires honest assessment of skills.
- **D) Correct.** A scope of practice requires therapists to practice within the laws of the state, but only states determine if a license to practice massage is required.

47.
- **A) Correct.** Asking a client about his symptoms using OL' DR. FICARA allows the therapist to find out information such as when the symptoms began, their frequency, and other descriptors.
- B) Incorrect. The Objective portion is what is observed by the therapist.
- C) Incorrect. The Assessment portion describes what type of treatment was provided to the client.
- D) Incorrect. The Plan portion notes homework for the client and describes future treatments.

48.
- **A) Correct.** Cold, tingling, burning, and numbness are the client's responses to cryotherapy.
- B) Incorrect. The client should not feel twinging and should definitely not blister from cryotherapy.
- C) Incorrect. The client should not twitch from the cryotherapy treatment.
- D) Incorrect. The client should definitely not experience nerve damage from proper cryotherapy application. Therapists should review contraindications and perform thorough intake with clients before treatment.

49.
- A) Incorrect. Kyphosis is an overdeveloped thoracic curve that may result from a muscular imbalance, osteoporosis, or ankylosing spondylitis.
- B) Incorrect. Lordosis is an overexaggerated lumbar curve resulting from muscle imbalance, muscle weakness, and the vulnerability of the spine to stress and pressure placed on it by the rest of the body.
- **C) Correct.** Gout is a form of arthritis that is the result of excess uric acid and causes inflammation in the lower legs and feet.

    D) Incorrect. Scoliosis is a curvature of the spine (most frequently to the right).

50. **A)** Incorrect. The cardiac muscle's function is to pump blood.

    B) Incorrect. There is no muscle type named *neuromuscular*.

    C) Incorrect. Skeletal muscle produces skeletal movement.

    D) **Correct.** Smooth muscle surrounds hollow internal organs.

51. **A)** Incorrect. I bands are thin filaments on sarcomeres.

    B) **Correct.** The *t* in t-tubules stands for *transverse*.

    C) Incorrect. The zone of overlap is where thin and thick filaments overlap each other.

    D) Incorrect. Myosin is a type of myofibril.

52. **A)** **Correct.** Therapists are never allowed to prescribe or diagnose, as these actions are beyond their scope of practice.

    B) Incorrect. Therapists can never diagnose or prescribe because these were not included in their education.

    C) Incorrect. A therapist should never diagnose or prescribe but instead refer a client to a doctor.

    D) Incorrect. A therapist cannot diagnose or prescribe and should tell the client to wait for the doctor's input.

53. **A)** Incorrect. Agreeing to move from the reception area to a massage room is not the best example of implied consent.

    B) **Correct.** Filling out an intake form and signing it is considered implied consent.

    C) Incorrect. A client who agrees to a treatment plan after discussion with a therapist is giving informed consent.

    D) Incorrect. Disrobing before a massage happens after informed consent is given to the therapist.

54. **A)** Incorrect. The three layers of the meninges are the pia mater, arachnoid, and dura mater.

    B) Incorrect. Meninges protect the brain and spinal cord.

    C) **Correct.** The blood-brain barrier separates blood and cerebrospinal fluid.

    D) Incorrect. The central nervous system consists of the brain and spinal cord.

55. **A)** Incorrect. This aspect absorbs neurotransmitters.

    B) Incorrect. This aspect emits neurotransmitters.

    C) Incorrect. Nodes of Ranvier are gaps on myelinated axons.

    D) **Correct.** The synaptic cleft is located between the pre- and post-synapse.

56. **A)** Incorrect. The cerebrum is the largest region of the brain.

    B) Incorrect. The cerebellum regulates motor movements.

    C) **Correct.** Neuroglia are cells that support and protect neurons.

    D) Incorrect. The diencephalon houses the thalamus and hypothalamus.

57. **A)** Incorrect. Twenty to thirty percent of semen comes from the prostate gland.

    B) Incorrect. Ten percent of semen comes from bulbourethral glands.

    C) Incorrect. Sperm is produced in the testes.

    D) **Correct.** Most semen is made up of fluid from the seminal vesicles.

58. **A)** Incorrect. Friction is more superficial, using the therapist's fingers or thumbs; cross-fiber uses the therapist's digital pressure to move superficial structures against deeper ones.

    B) Incorrect. Friction and cross-fiber friction are both performed with a therapist's fingers and thumbs.

    C) **Correct.** Friction is a more superficial technique, while cross-fiber uses superficial tissues to scrub against deeper tissues.

    D) Incorrect. Friction is a more superficial technique, while cross-fiber uses superficial tissues to scrub against deeper tissues.

59.
- A) Incorrect. Cortisol is a stress hormone.
- B) Incorrect. Relaxin is a hormone released in pregnant women to prepare their bodies to deliver.
- **C) Correct.** Oxytocin is known as the *cuddle hormone*, promoting a feeling of well-being.
- D) Incorrect. Dopamine plays a role in starting motion.

60.
- A) Incorrect. *Valvular veins* is not a real term.
- **B) Correct.** Varicose veins develop when veins' valves do not close properly, causing a backflow and pooling of blood in the veins. They are unsightly and sometimes uncomfortable for clients.
- C) Incorrect. Lymphatic beds, or capillary beds, are where blood changes over from ingoing to outgoing properties.
- D) Incorrect. Spider veins are a cosmetic issue that can sometimes be a precursor to varicose veins.

61.
- A) Incorrect. Therapists should always take a moment before a massage begins to clear their mind and direct their focus on the client.
- B) Incorrect. The therapist can use this time to move the client into a relaxed and comfortable state of mind.
- C) Incorrect. How first touch is perceived by a client is important and can set the tone for the massage.
- **D) Correct.** A therapist should not bring a cell phone into a massage session.

62.
- A) Incorrect. SOAP notes can be shared in court cases when applicable.
- B) Incorrect. SOAP notes can be shared with a client's doctor to ensure the client receives the best comprehensive care for her condition.
- **C) Correct.** SOAP notes should not be shared outside of medical or legal spaces with people unrelated to the client's care or case.
- D) Incorrect. SOAP notes can be shared with another massage therapist who also sees the client.

63.
- **A) Correct.** A Baker's cyst is also known as a popliteal cyst because it appears behind the knee.
- B) Incorrect. A ganglion cyst is a small connective tissue pouch filled with fluid that forms around the joints.
- C) Incorrect. A lipoma is a benign fatty tumor encased in connective tissue.
- D) Incorrect. A wart is a small tumor that arises from the epidermis and is viral in nature.

64.
- A) Incorrect. Acupressure uses pressure applied to energy pathways.
- B) Incorrect. Shiatsu is a Japanese modality similar to acupressure.
- **C) Correct.** Healing touch is a form of energy work that does not use pressure.
- D) Incorrect. Trigger point work focuses on myofascial points using compressions.

65.
- A) Incorrect. Luteinizing hormone assists with the maturation of oocytes.
- **B) Correct.** Estrogen keeps the endometrium richly supplied with blood in the event of pregnancy.
- C) Incorrect. Progesterone creates a barrier to deter sperm movement after pregnancy occurs.
- D) Incorrect. Luteinizing hormone triggers ovulation.

66.
- A) Incorrect. Kneading is a Swedish massage technique.
- B) Incorrect. Gliding is a Swedish massage technique.
- C) Incorrect. Vibration is a Swedish massage technique.
- **D) Correct.** Joint mobilization is a Swedish gymnastic technique.

67.
- A) Incorrect. The trachea is commonly referred to as the windpipe.
- B) Incorrect. The pharynx is commonly referred to as the throat.

	C)	**Correct.** The larynx contains the vocal cords that vibrate as air passes.
	D)	Incorrect. The frontal sinus is one of the air spaces that open into the nasal cavity.
68.	A)	Incorrect. Employers will provide therapists with a written job description and duties.
	B)	Incorrect. Employers will provide therapists with a written or video presentation of procedures.
	C)	Incorrect. Expectations of professional conduct will be communicated by an employer or prospective employer.
	D)	**Correct.** Many employers discourage sexual relationships between coworkers outside of work, especially between employees of different ranks.
69.	A)	Incorrect. Hydraulic tables are not submerged in water.
	B)	Incorrect. Stationary tables can be moved when a client is not on them.
	C)	**Correct.** Hydraulic tables can be raised or lowered when a client is on them, with the press of a button.
	D)	Incorrect. Stationary tables can only be adjusted when a client is not on them.
70.	A)	Incorrect. The epiglottis is a lid-like piece of cartilage that covers the trachea.
	B)	Incorrect. Alveolar sacs are located at the end of each bronchiole.
	C)	Incorrect. Cilia are microscopic hairs in the upper respiratory system.
	D)	**Correct.** The trachea has a number of c-shaped rings that keep the trachea from collapsing.
71.	A)	Incorrect. During expiration, the diaphragm relaxes.
	B)	Incorrect. During inspiration, the diaphragm contracts.
	C)	**Correct.** The diaphragm separates the thoracic cavity from the abdominal cavity.
	D)	Incorrect. Alveoli are found in the lungs.

72.	A)	Incorrect. Zero balancing is a modality that incorporates energy flow and body structures.
	B)	Incorrect. Stones may be heated in water but this modality is not water based.
	C)	**Correct.** *Watsu* means water shiatsu and is a water-based treatment.
	D)	Incorrect. Esalen is a modality developed in the 1960s that does not incorporate water.
73.	A)	Incorrect. Ashiatsu is a technique to provide deep pressure using the feet.
	B)	Incorrect. Rolfing is soft tissue manipulation.
	C)	Incorrect. Sports massage may incorporate techniques that are deep and vigorous.
	D)	**Correct.** Craniosacral is considered a light touch modality safe for all ages.
74.	A)	Incorrect. Salt and sugar scrubs are common in spas.
	B)	**Correct.** Hot waxing is a practice performed by aestheticians.
	C)	Incorrect. Water used to prepare hot and cold treatments used in massage is acceptable.
	D)	Incorrect. Herbal products may be infused or incorporated into massage applications.
75.	A)	**Correct.** Osseous tissue is highly vascular, not dead.
	B)	Incorrect. Cartilage is firm but flexible and found throughout the body.
	C)	Incorrect. Ligaments are fibrous and elastic and are a bone-to-bone attachment.
	D)	Incorrect. Marrow is soft and spongy and is a mix of red and yellow in adults.
76.	A)	**Correct.** Clients disclose medical information all the time. Why should this be different?
	B)	Incorrect. This response is inappropriate; the therapist should not assume he or she is now a trusted confidant of the client.

	C)	Incorrect. This action violates numerous codes and standards of conduct and is a stereotypical response to this medical condition.		D)	Incorrect. Parasites are considered pathogens that attempt to enter the body.
	D)	Incorrect. This would be a clear violation of boundaries as well as an insensitive thing to say to any client.	81.	A)	Incorrect. Genetic influences begin at conception.
77.	A)	Incorrect. Endangerment sites are related to arteries, veins, and body organs.		B)	Incorrect. Allergic reactions result from an overexposure to a pathogen.
				C)	Incorrect. The hygiene hypothesis suggests that birth order affects the development of the immune system.
	B)	Incorrect. Pain related to pressure generally indicates muscle and soft tissue tenderness.		D)	**Correct.** Immune cells attacking themselves results in an autoimmune disease.
	C)	**Correct.** Knowing the location of prominent bony landmarks can help locate muscle sites.	82.	**A)**	**Correct.** When the urethra receives urine, urination occurs.
	D)	Incorrect. Osteoporosis is a diagnosis made by a physician.		B.)	Incorrect. The bladder empties into the urethra.
78.	A)	Incorrect. Hematopoiesis has nothing to do with diseases of the blood.		C)	Incorrect. The ureters are tubes that route urine from the kidneys to the bladder.
	B)	Incorrect. There is no long bone part named the hematopoiesis.		D)	Incorrect. Urine passes through the ureters and bladder before urination occurs.
	C)	**Correct.** Blood cells are produced in the marrow.	83.	A)	Incorrect. There needs to be a 3:1 application in order to produce greater benefits.
	D)	Incorrect. That condition is osteoporosis.			
79.	A)	Incorrect. The height of the therapist is a determining factor for adjusting the table height.		B)	Incorrect. Cold therapy should be applied for a shorter amount of time so as not to erase the benefits of hot therapy.
	B)	Incorrect. The weight of the client is a determining factor for adjusting the table height.		C)	Incorrect. Heat is applied longer than cold is.
	C)	**Correct.** The height of the client is not a determining factor for adjusting the table height.		**D)**	**Correct.** A three-minute heat application to a one-minute cold application should be used.
	D)	Incorrect. Depending on the type of massage treatment, the therapist may prefer variations in table height.	84.	**A)**	**Correct.** Ling created the Swedish movement cure.
80.	A)	Incorrect. Viruses are considered pathogens that attempt to enter the body.		B)	Incorrect. Johann Mezger, a Dutch physician, incorporated massage into physical rehabilitation after Ling's death.
	B)	Incorrect. Fungi are considered pathogens that attempt to enter the body.		C)	Incorrect. The Taylor brothers opened an orthopedic practice in the United States after studying the Swedish movement cure.
	C)	**Correct.** Cellular debris is what remains of broken-down cells.			

    D) Incorrect. Douglas O. Graham wrote *A Practical Treatise on Massage*.

85. **A) Correct.** Accidently running into a client in a grocery store is a communal dual relationship.
    B) Incorrect. A social dual relationship occurs between a therapist and acquaintances, friends of friends, friends of family members, and people the therapist knows through affiliations and memberships.
    C) Incorrect. The client is neither a family member nor a close friend.
    D) Incorrect. A work-based dual relationship is massaging a coworker, supervisor, or owner of the business that employs the therapist.

86. A) Incorrect. OSHA does work to save lives by promoting safe work environments.
    B) Incorrect. OSHA does work to prevent injuries by promoting safe work environments.
    C) Correct. OSHA does not protest inequality.
    D) Incorrect. OSHA does work to protect the health of American workers through establishing safety guidelines.

87. **A) Correct.** The suffix –*plegia* means paralysis.
    B) Incorrect. Emphysema affects the ability of the lungs to exchange gases because of damaged or destroyed alveoli.
    C) Incorrect. Cystic fibrosis causes the production of thick mucus, hindering the intake of air in the respiratory tract and the absorption of nutrients in the digestive tract.
    D) Incorrect. Asthma occurs when the smooth muscle of the bronchial tubes spasms and constricts in response to an allergen, stress, or inflammation, hindering breathing and resulting in excessive mucus production.

88. **A) Correct.** Cirrhosis can be caused by fatty deposits related or unrelated to alcohol abuse, and by hepatitis B and C.
    B) Incorrect. Celiac disease is indicated by intestinal inflammation, damage, and destruction of intestinal villi upon consumption of gluten. This damage also interferes with the digestion of nutrients.
    C) Incorrect. Cellulitis is a bacterial skin infection that can affect both the lymphatic and circulatory systems.
    D) Incorrect. Grave's disease is an autoimmune disorder that causes thyroid-producing hormones to be overproduced.

89. A) Incorrect. Vasodilation is a benefit of hot therapy.
    B) Correct. Vasoconstriction occurs with the application of cold therapy.
    C) Incorrect. Hot therapy increases blood and lymph flow to the area.
    D) Incorrect. Hot therapy decreases nerve firings of the area applied.

90. A) Incorrect. Once waste is classified as urine, it needs to reach the bladder before the urge to urinate occurs.
    B) Incorrect. Ureters only transport.
    C) Correct. Once the bladder fills, receptors in the bladder wall communicate the urge to urinate.
    D) Incorrect. While removal of waste is important to the maintenance of blood pH, it has nothing to do with communicating the urge to urinate.

91. A) Incorrect. Therapists should never leave the room during hot therapy applications.
    B) Incorrect. Therapists should take care of personal needs before and after treatments, and they should never leave the client alone during the treatment.
    C) Correct. Therapists should always be in the room during a treatment.
    D) Incorrect. Therapists should stay in the room and continue the treatment after the first application.

92.
- A) Incorrect. This type of conversation is not acceptable at all in the workplace.
- B) Incorrect. Management will not consider this appropriate and will want to take further action beyond disallowing the therapist to perform massages on this client again.
- **C) Correct.** The employer will prepare a written explanation of why the behavior was inappropriate and have the therapist sign it.
- D) Incorrect. If the coworker did this, he or she would be in violation as well.

93.
- A) Incorrect. Ayurveda has no relationship to the three treasures.
- B) Incorrect. Yin/Yang is a belief that all things are interconnected and inseparable.
- C) Incorrect. Shiatsu is a treatment developed in Japan.
- **D) Correct.** Qi, shen, and jing are called the three treasures in traditional Chinese medicine.

94.
- A) Incorrect. It is best for sheets and towels to be washed at a high temperature to stop the spread of infections through pathogens.
- **B) Correct.** Hot water kills pathogens that can spread infection or disease.
- C) Incorrect. While cold water may be better for the environment, spreading infections through pathogens is not safe for the client or the therapist.
- D) Incorrect. Cold water may treat stains better, but hot water kills pathogens that spread infection.

95.
- A) Incorrect. The body has multiple bursae, or connective tissue sacs filled with synovial fluid. Bursitis is an inflammation of these sacs.
- B) Incorrect. A dislocation occurs when the articulating bones that form a joint separate.
- C) Incorrect. Trigeminal neuralgia is extreme nerve pain marked by sensations of burning and electrical impulses in the lower face and jaw.
- **D) Correct.** Adhesive capsulitis occurs in the synovial joint capsule at the glenohumeral joint and is preceded by a condition that causes inflammation. As it progresses, the joint capsule begins to adhere to bone, ultimately limiting range of motion in the shoulder.

96.
- A) Incorrect. In Ayurveda, the eight pillars refer to eight steps related to a good health regime.
- B) Incorrect. Ayurveda means life knowledge.
- C) Incorrect. In Ayurveda, doshas play a part in assessment and treatment.
- **D) Correct.** Acupressure points are related to traditional Chinese medicine practices.

97.
- A) Incorrect. Healing touch is a light touch therapy.
- **B) Correct.** There are seven chakras that are considered energy channels.
- C) Incorrect. Polarity therapy is a light touch therapy.
- D) Incorrect. Acupressure is a practice that applies pressure to acupressure points.

98.
- A) Incorrect. Hartvig Nissen wrote a paper entitled "Swedish Movement and Massage."
- B) Incorrect. Charles Fayette Taylor and his brother published the first textbook on Ling's Swedish movement cure.
- **C) Correct.** *The Art of Massage* was published in 1896.
- D) Incorrect. Ling developed The Swedish movement cure but did not publish a book.

99.
- A) Incorrect. The therapist should disinfect the treatment room before and after each treatment.
- **B) Correct.** The massage room should be disinfected before and after each client.
- C) Incorrect. The room should be disinfected before and after each treatment, but a deep clean is a good idea every week or so.

- D) Incorrect. The treatment room needs to be disinfected on a regular basis, before and after each treatment.

100.
- A) Incorrect. Impetigo is a highly contagious infection caused by staphylococcus and streptococcus bacteria.
- B) Incorrect. Phlebitis is the inflammation of a vein usually caused by a trauma or damage to blood vessel walls, inhibited venous flow, and abnormal blood coagulation factors.
- **C) Correct.** Tinea is a lesion caused by a fungal infection and is generically referred to as ringworm.
- D) Incorrect. A varicose vein is a superficial vein that has become twisted and swollen.

Made in United States
Orlando, FL
20 July 2022